SUGAR FLOWERS
Revised Edition

SUGAR FLOWERS

Revised Edition

Over 1 000 easy 'look and learn' illustrations
for the creation of gum paste flowers for
cake decorating.

JILL MAYTHAM

Published by Jem Publishers
P.O. Box 115, Kloof,
Natal 3640
South Africa
© Copyright 1987 Jem Publishers
© Copyright Revised Edition 1994 Jem Publishers

ISBN 0-620-10977-7

1st Edition July 1987
2nd Edition November 1987
3rd Edition July 1988
4th Edition October 1990
Revised Edition January 1994
Revised Edition July 1998

Typeset & Reproduction by Hirt & Carter
Photography: Shawn Driman
Printed and Bound by Interpak

FOREWORD

This is not just another cake decorating book. Rather it is an excellent guide for people wanting to know the finer points of flower modelling.

Many of us have felt the need for expert advice and clear step-by-step instructions in this field. Now, at last, we have this book, with a wealth of information on the modelling of over sixty flowers as well as the making of corsages and bouquets.

This LOOK and LEARN approach is a very modern, quick and effective method of conveying knowledge to the reader. With very little time at our disposal, we don't often have the opportunity to peruse and read long descriptions and explanations on how to make a flower. The superb line drawings accompanied by precise and brief instructions is the ultimate answer.

Jill Maytham with her background of teaching Cake Decorating and Sugar Art, and also being a successful exhibitor, is well qualified to produce a work of this calibre. She has the standing and the knowledge to give meaning and interest to this fascinating subject.

It is my special privilege to recommend this book to the beginner as well as to the advanced cake decorator.

Gladiola Botha.

PREFACE

In this book, a simple 'look and learn' approach to making flowers from gum paste is set out both for the beginner and the more experienced decorator.

There are many methods of constructing flowers for cake decorating which produce equally pleasing results. Experimentation is encouraged to stimulate the creative imagination of the decorator.

It is my hope that the cake decorator will benefit from this book, finding pleasure and satisfaction in the creation of sugar flowers.

DEDICATION

For their love and encouragement, patience and understanding, this book is dedicated to Neil, my husband, and to Emily and Michael, my children.

For their interest and encouragement in all the many challenges life has offered me, this book is also dedicated to my parents, Murray and Joan McLachlan.

Psalm 147:1

Praise the Lord!
For it is good to sing
praises to our God;
for He is gracious, and a song of
praise is seemly.

ACKNOWLEDGEMENTS

I wish to record my indebtedness to the late Connie Swanepoel, who was my first teacher.

Special thanks and appreciation to Val Bannister, Diana Edgcumbe, Anne Hancock, Lesley Konigkramer, Pam Milne and Jillyan Mourant, all of whom gave me invaluable help in the making of the flowers and foliage which appear in the photographs.

Thanks also to Laurel Cook who drew and re-drew the illustrations. Very special thanks to Valda Luby for proof-reading the script, and for helping with the layout of the flowers in the photographs.

Many others, too numerous to mention, who in any way helped this book reach finality, are also thanked.

Finally, I commend to the readers of this book the South African Cake Decorators Guild, which encourages the highest workmanship amongst its members. It also provides opportunities in the competitive field, stimulating interest in this art form.

Jill Maytham

PHOTOGRAPHS

All the flowers and foliage featured in the photographs in this book have been made out of sugar. Each flower appearing in the instructions in this book can be found in the photographs.

The frog and the driftwood have also been made out of sugar.

NOTE:

JEM Cutters and Tools have been used exclusively in the creation of the flowers and foliage illustrated in this book.

CONTENTS

CONTENTS

$\mathcal{R}$emember . . .

* You are working with food!

* Wash your hands before you begin, and frequently as you proceed.

* Keep all your equipment clean.

* Keep your flower paste sealed in a plastic bag placed in a plastic container with a lid. Each colour should be in a separate bag.

* Store flower paste in the fridge if not in use.

* Before beginning to make a flower, 'work' paste thoroughly to ensure that it is pliable.

* Paste should stretch and not crumble.

* If paste is too dry, add a little egg white to it.

* If paste is too sticky, a little white vegetable fat rubbed on your hands should help.

* Only use authentic non-toxic food colouring to colour flower paste.

* Never use old flower paste. If it has a sour smell, it will not dry!

* Never use old gelatin to mix flower paste. It discolours the paste.

* Never roll out too much paste. Roll out only sufficient for the petals you need to cut out.

* A variety of worktop surfaces are suitable – panelite board, glass or a ceramic tile are a few suggestions.

* Work in a good light.

* A table lamp will help to hasten the drying time your work needs.

* It is preferable to shade petals, foliage etc., in the daylight.

* Food colouring petal dust should be used to shade petals and foliage in preference to non-toxic water colours or chalks.

* Mix petal dust with alcohol for painting on flowers or foliage.

* N.B. BECAUSE SOMETHING IS NON-TOXIC, THIS DOES *NOT* MEAN THAT IT IS EDIBLE. All shading of flowers and foliage should be done in moderation.

* Too much liquid colouring applied to finished flower will cause petals, etc., to dissolve.

* When cutting out your paste, jiggle the cutter to ensure a clean cutting edge.

* When using a large cutter, apply even pressure over its total area to ensure achieving a clean edge.

* If paste should stick in a cutter, use a pin to lift out the petal or foliage.

* Keep cutters scrupulously clean to avoid flower paste sticking in them.

* The impression of the tool you are using should not remain visible on the surface of your work.

* Soften the edges of petals with your fingers.

* When veining against a veiner, press the 'dry' side of the paste you have rolled and cut out against the veiner – i.e. the upper side.

* If dry petals have a rough edge, use an emery board to neaten finish.

* Store finished work in a sealed container. Ensure that both are thoroughly dry before storing.

* When arranging flowers on a cake, NEVER push wires into the icing. This is most unhygienic and should be remembered at all times!

* A base may be made for the arrangement of your flowers by using a little 'platform' of fondant if you do not wish to make a bouquet or spray.

* Wire may be omitted in the structure of flowers or foliage if preferred.

* When frilling or fluting petals, pick up the petal constantly to enable it to stretch. This will create the frilled effect desired.

* Work paste through at least once a week if not in use. This will prolong its' 'life'.

* There are several ways to make the same flower. Find the simplest method to suit yourself.

NOTE: 'Cloud' referred to in the instructions is the synthetic fibre used for filling duvets. Another suggestion is small pieces of sponge foam which have been cut to suitable size.

NOTE: The fine fuse wire referred to in the book is gauge 0.3 and 0.4.

*H*elpful *H*ints

* If you live in humid conditions, a cupboard with an electric light bulb fitted in the base is an excellent way to store and preserve flowers or foliage. The cupboard should have small vent holes at the top to allow the hot air to escape.

* Silica gel helps to a small degree to keep flowers dry. If you use this method, watch the silica gel as, when it changes colour, it should be reheated in a cool oven to restore its function.

* Roll paste out between light plastic sheets (about the thickness of a bank bag).

* When colouring your work, the addition of a drop or two of dish-washing liquid to the small quantity of water required for cleaning your brush will help the paint to adhere to the petals and foliage. The soap content removes the slightly greasy finish these may have.

* For the best effect, roll paste thinly to create a lifelike appearance.

* If your hands perspire, dust them with baby powder. This will help keep them cool and dry. Working on a Jem Petal Pad will help alleviate this problem.

* Make your own pollen by using a mixture of maize meal and petal dust. If you wish to have a shimmering effect, use castor sugar mixed with a little petal dust.

* The new pearly petal dusts are attractive on certain flowers if used sparingly, e.g. orchids.

* If you wish to create a 'drop of water' effect on your work, simply dissolve a little clear gelatin and carefully release a single drop on to the petal etc.

* For a sand effect, mix colourless gelatin with some cocoa and any small broken bits of icing you may have.

* Use a little liquid colouring or petal dust on a toothbrush to create a speckled effect by brushing your thumb over the toothbrush. Before applying to the leaf, test the result on a piece of paper to ensure that the right quantity of colours is on the brush to achieve the desired effect.

* Steam will remove the chalky effect from petals caused by petal dust. Push the wire stems of the flowers or foliage into some covered oasis to act as a barrier between the steam and your hand to prevent burning yourself. Hold the flowers or leaf in the steam about 20 cm away from the kettle. The moisture will remove the dull effect, giving the petals a life-like appearance. Excess cornflour will also disappear using this method.

* Cover oasis for dry flower arrangements with plastic cling wrap to avoid particles of oasis making contact with your hands or the gum paste.

* Substitute egg white with gum glue made from Tylose C1000p. This has the benefit of not going off. See recipe on Page 232.

* When taping wire allow ± an extra 1 cm of florist tape to double back on the wire. This will prevent the tape from becoming unravelled.

* When painting 'dots' on to petals a cocktail stick is easier to use than a paint brush, as it does not bend.

Jem Tools

1A Small ball tool. Useful to press into blossom petals resting on foam, creating a cupped effect.

1A

1B When using flower paste to cover sprigs and other stems which have more than one branch, this tool will help to smooth the stems.

1B

2A A blunt ended point which may be used to begin making a trumpet shaped flower. It is also used to indent baby blossom petals resting on foam.

2A

2B This is a fluting tool which will frill the edge of petals.

2B

3A A very useful tool to smooth petals on the palm of your hand, or to encourage petals to curl when used on a foam surface. Use as a ball tool.

3A

3B As for 3A, except a slightly smaller head.

3B

4A A most useful tool for fluting and frilling petals. This tool will also help to increase the size of any petal. Its' pointed tip is used to emphasize the centre of some flowers.

4A

4B This is a veining tool, which will make vein markings difficult to create with other veiners.

4B

5A This tool is used to form trumpet flowers.

5A

5B The single edge of this tool may be used to make the Garrett frill. The double edge of the tool is used to mark in veins on daisy petals.

5B

6A A large ball tool for use on larger petals.

6A

6B A shell impression which is useful to indent the edge of a plaque made out of fondant or pastillage. Also the edges of a cake board covered with fondant may be decorated using this pattern.

6B

Jem Tools

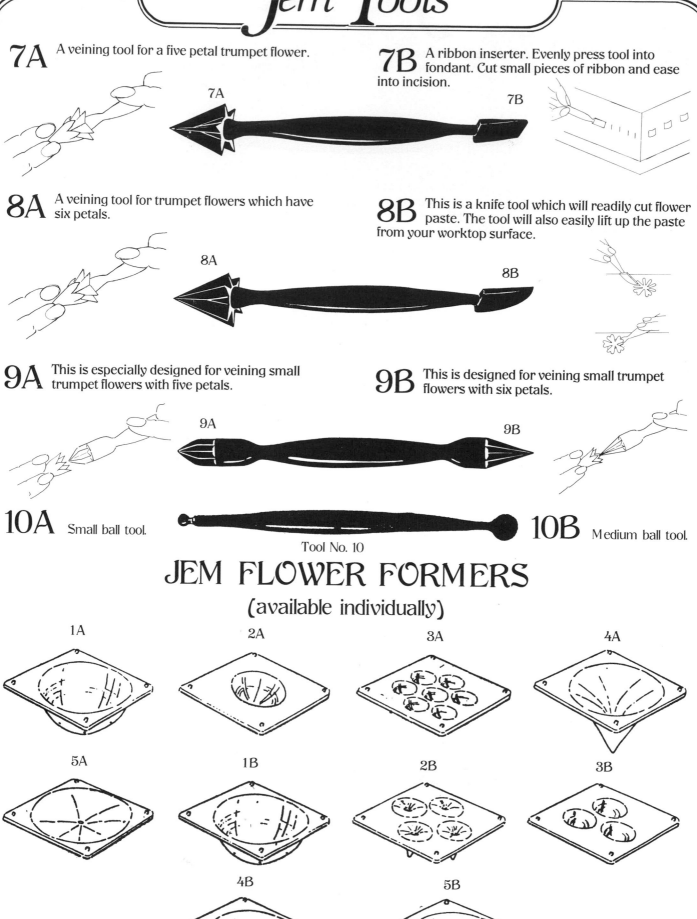

7A A veining tool for a five petal trumpet flower.

7B A ribbon inserter. Evenly press tool into fondant. Cut small pieces of ribbon and ease into incision.

8A A veining tool for trumpet flowers which have six petals.

8B This is a knife tool which will readily cut flower paste. The tool will also easily lift up the paste from your worktop surface.

9A This is especially designed for veining small trumpet flowers with five petals.

9B This is designed for veining small trumpet flowers with six petals.

10A Small ball tool.

Tool No. 10

10B Medium ball tool.

JEM FLOWER FORMERS
(available individually)

1A

2A

3A

4A

5A

1B

2B

3B

4B

5B

4

The Handy Holder

(Supplied with 10 Jem flower Formers)

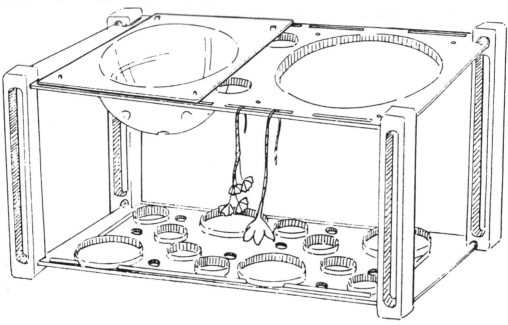

Flowers formers clip into position.

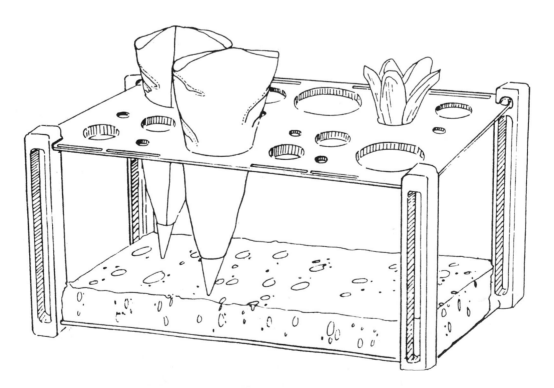

Upside down, the Handy Holder serves as an icing bag support with the tip of the nozzle resting on dampened sponge foam to prevent icing drying.

Tape Cutter

Note: * Blades may be removed by unscrewing side of tape cutter.
* Blades can be turned around when blunt.
* Make sure blades are replaced evenly, or cutter will not work properly. Before tightening screws, lightly tap tape cutter on table.

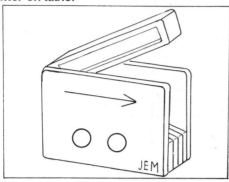

1 Lift up centre piece (shutter) – it is removable.

2 Thread required length of florist tape, or ribbon, from behind centre piece. Close shutter. Apply gentle pressure to centre piece and, using other hand, pull florist tape or ribbon through. Illustration shows tape cut in half and two quarter widths. Remove one blade to cut the tape in half and the other half into quarters.

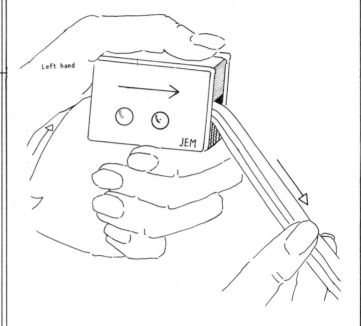

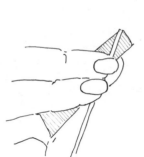

3 To cover wire, place wire at an angle on the tape.

4 Secure tape to wire.

5 Hold wire between thumb and index finger in left hand. Allow tape to be guided by right hand and gently twist wire between thumb and index finger. Allow tape to stretch. Allow ± an extra 1 cm of florist tape to double back on wire. This will help prevent the unravelling of the tape.

Arum Lily

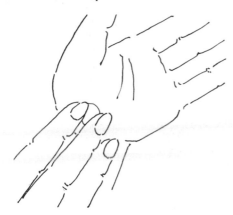

Note: The use of crêpe paper shown in this flower is optional.

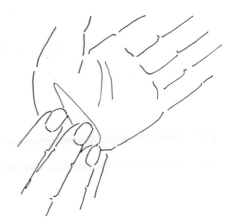

1 Roll out a ball of yellow paste about the size of a marble.

2 Roll it backwards and forwards on the palm of your hand, forming a pointed tip and a rounded base.

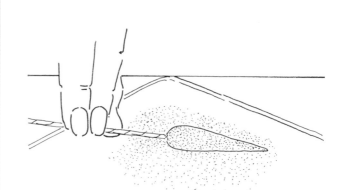

3 Using a piece of taped wire, gauge No 22, place gum glue on the top of the wire and then gently ease it into the spadix.

4 Place a little 'pollen' (white maize meal) on a flat surface and gently roll spadix in the pollen.

5 Using white vegetable fat, lightly grease worktop surface. Select cutter size required, (Cutter shown, No B42), cut out spathe in colour of your choice.

B42

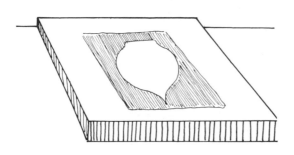

6 Place a small piece of white crêpe paper on work surface – make sure the grain of the paper is parallel to the shape of the point of the petal. Place petal over crêpe paper.

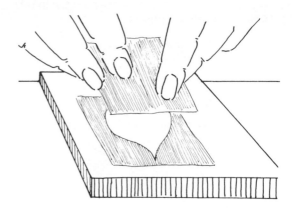

7 Using another piece of crêpe paper, place over top of petal.

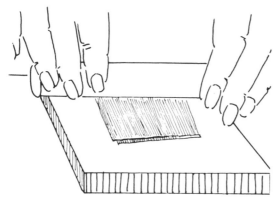

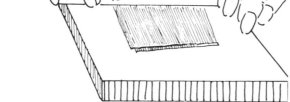

8 Very carefully roll out petal. The crêpe paper will give it an excellent veined effect. (Sometimes the icing paste tends to stick to new crêpe paper – a little vegetable fat on the paper will help).

9 Place egg white or gum glue on the spathe as indicated in the sketch.

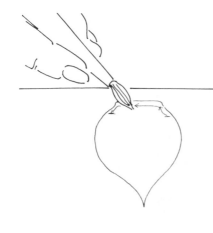

10 Place the spadix in the centre of the spathe and overlap the spathe, allowing the petal to curl slightly backwards.

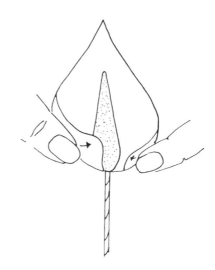

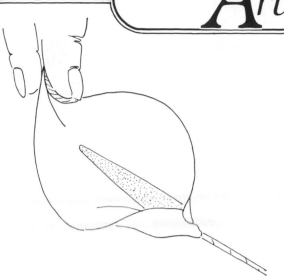

11 Gently press tip of petal between fingers to give it a curl. Stand in oasis or something similar to dry.

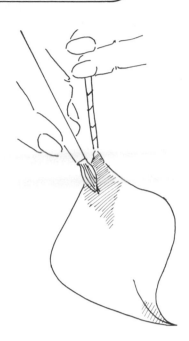

12 When flower is dry, lightly shade the back of petal with a pale green chalk.

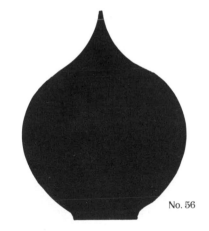

No. 56

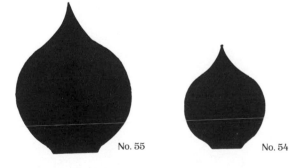

No. 55   No. 54

13 Alternative cutters, Nos 54, 55 and 56.

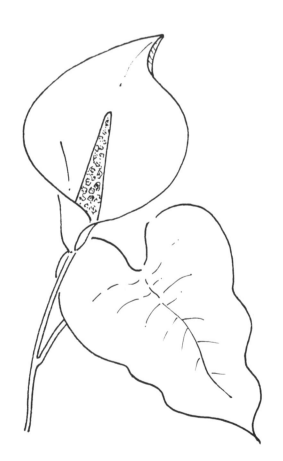

14 Finished flower.

Bell Flower

Note: Many flowers not specifically mentioned in this book may be formed by using this method.

Size 1   Size 2   Size 3   Size 4

No. 63   No. 64   No. 65   No. 66

Six Petal Daisy

1 Using flower paste, roll a small ball to suit the size of the cutter you will use.

2 Shape ball into pear shape.

3 Flatten outside edges.

4 Paste should look like a Mexican hat.

5 Place "Mexican hat" over the centre of the cutter.

6 Press fingers around edges of cutter, cutting the flower paste. Return surplus paste to plastic bag.

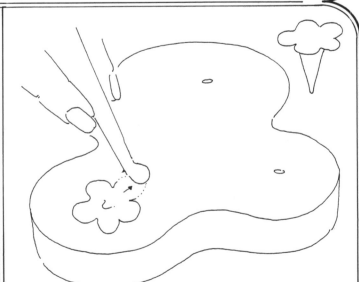

7 Place trumpet into Mexican Petal Pad and work petal edges using tool 3A or 10A until thin.

10

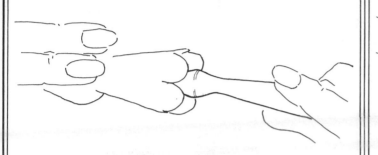

8 Using Tool No 2B, work tool into petals forming a deep throat.

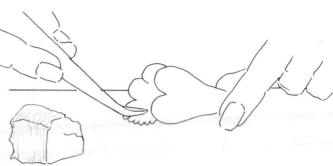

White vegetable fat

9 Rub a little white vegetable fat on worktop surface and, using spoon side of tool No 4A, gently 'flute' edges.

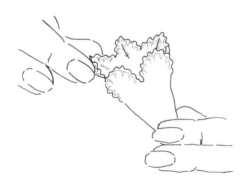

10 Using tips of fingers, gently shape petals.

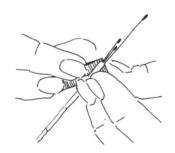

11 Using three stamens and fine florist wire, secure with florist tape.

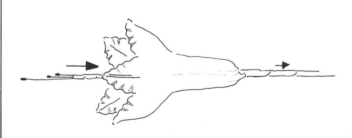

12 Gently ease stamens through centre of flower.

13 Finished flower showing stamens in position. A calyx could be added. Use either Cutter No 23 or B55, depending on the size of flower cutter in use.

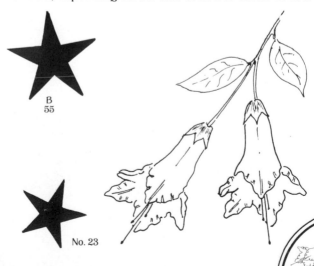

B 55

No. 23

Daisy

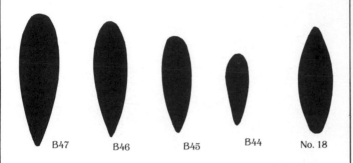

1 Cut out a number of petals at a time using one of any of the following cutters, No. 18 or B44; B45 or B46 or B47. Return surplus paste to plastic bag. Cover petals with plastic, or lid, to prevent petals from drying out.

B47   B46   B45   B44   No. 18

2 Place petals on foam. Using Tool No. 5B (double edge), gently press on petals to create a ridge.

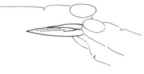

3 Using fingers, gently shape petals, creating a slightly pointed tip to petals.

4 Using Cutter No. B36, cut out calyx for daisy. Place calyx on upside-down flower support 1A or 2A. Or use flower support No. 2B in the concave position to make semi-open daisies.

5 Using gum glue, tip the centre of calyx.

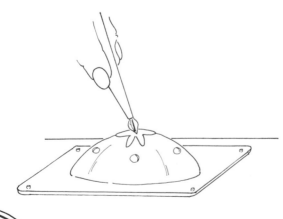

B36

Daisy

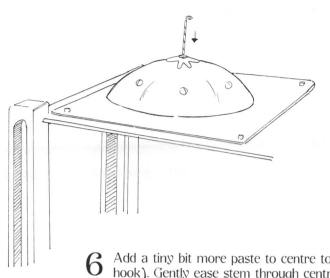

This cutter may be used to make this daisy. Mark and shape petals as illustrated in Step 2 and 3.

Eight Petal Daisy

6 Add a tiny bit more paste to centre to support stem (fine wire taped with a bent over flat hook). Gently ease stem through centre.

7 Using gum glue to secure, add petals to calyx one at a time.

8 Cut out more petals as needed – proceed as before and continue to increase petals on daisy until desired effect is achieved.

9 Make centre for daisy (see simple daisy instructions) and, using gum glue, place in centre of petals.

Use very small amounts of 'cloud' to lift petals, creating a natural effect.

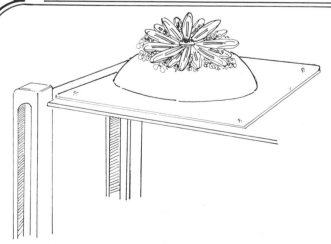

10 Finished daisy. Leaves on daisy stems should be taken from cutters No. L37, No. L20 or L23.

L20

L37

L23

Simple Daisy

1   Cut fine, taped, fuse wire. Form a small flat hook.

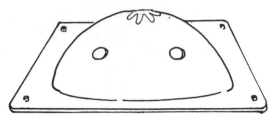

2   Using Cutter No. B36 or B37, cut out calyx in green paste and place over upside-down flower former 1A. Or use flower former 2A or 3B, depending on the size of the cutter, in the concave position.

B33

3   Now using either Cutter No. B35, B34 or B33, cut out the flower.

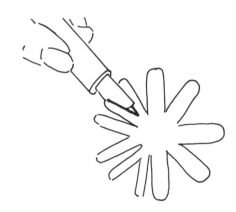

4   Using a sharp knife, slit each petal in half.

5   Using tool No. 4A, press into each petal, causing the petal to slightly flatten.

6   Place petals over calyx on upside-down petal support 1A, or in flower support 2A in normal position.

Gently ease hooked wire into centre of petals, and through the calyx.

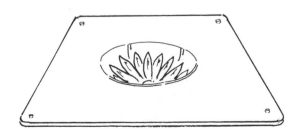

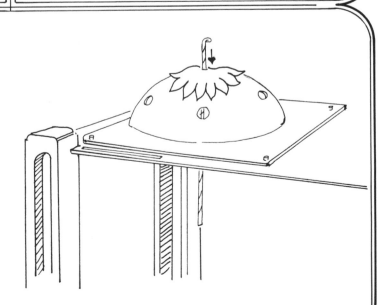

7 Using gum glue or egg white, paint over centre of hooked wire.

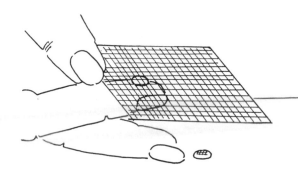

8 Press a tiny piece of paste against tulle or wire netting. This creates stamen effect.

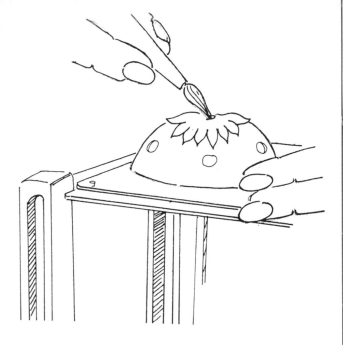

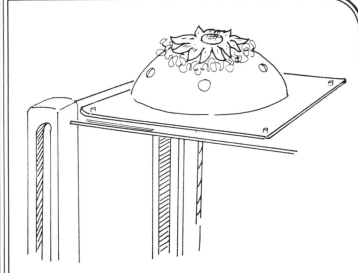

9 Place centre of flower in position. Prop up petals with a little 'cloud' to give daisy a good shape.

10 Finished daisy. Use L20 for leaf.

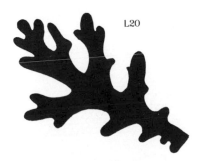

L20

Easy *Daisy*

B40

1 Using Cutter No. 13 or B40, cut out petals. Cover with soft plastic to prevent drying.

2 Place on a flower nail, and, using a sharp knife, slit each petal from the centre to the outside of the petals.

3 Using tweezers, gently press each petal together. The tweezers will create a fine ridge on the petals, making them look lifelike.

4 Place petals over convex former No. 1A. Gently ease taped, flat hooked, wire into centre of petals.

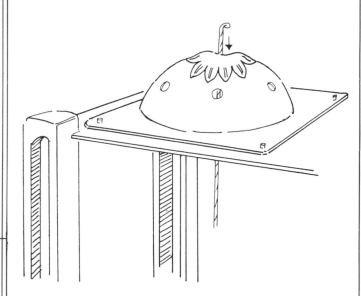

Alternatively use flower former No. 3B in the concave position. Add taped wire as described above.

5 Take a very small piece of paste and press against tulle or wire netting to create stamen effect.

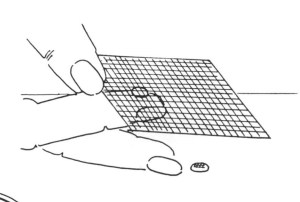

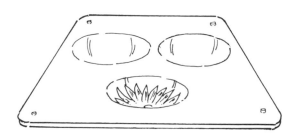

6 Apply gum glue over hooked wire and place centre of flower in position.

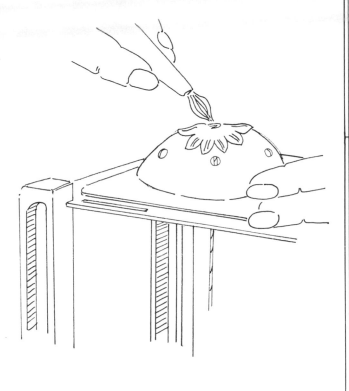

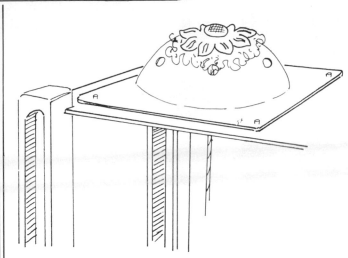

7 Use a little 'cloud' to lift up petals to improve shape of flower.

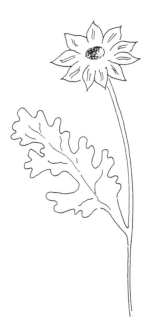

8 Finished daisy.
Use leaf L37, L20 or L23 for daisy leaf.

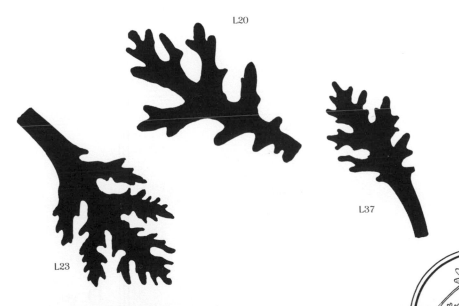

L20

L23

L37

Forget-me-not

Multiple Daisy Size 2

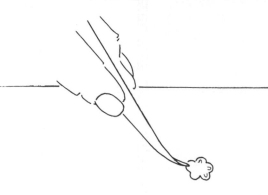

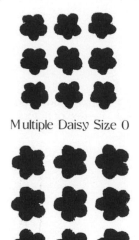

No. 67

Multiple Daisy Size 0

1 Using Cutter No. 67 and bright blue paste, cut out as many flowers as required. Cover them with soft plastic, or a plastic lid, to prevent drying.

Gently press tool 4A into each petal, causing a slight impression on each petal.

Multiple Daisy Size 1

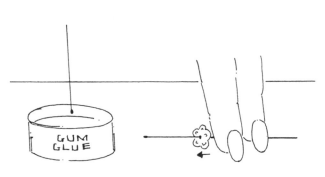

2 Dip stamen into gum glue.
Gently ease a stamen through centre of the flower. This flower appears to have a blue stamen.

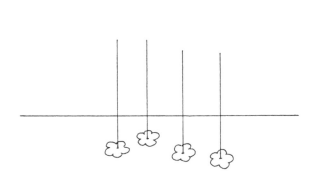

3 Allow flowers to dry upside down.

4 Using a minute piece of pale green paste, ease up stamen to form calyx.

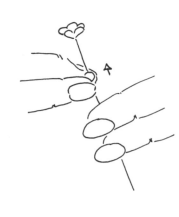

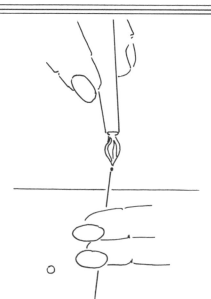

5 To make a bud, lightly tip a stamen with gum glue.

18

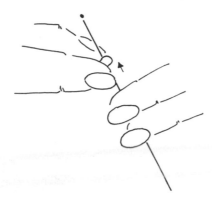

6 Using a tiny piece of coloured paste, ease on to stamen and shape into a bud. Light marks may be made with a sharp knife to create a petal division effect.

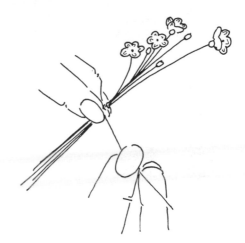

7 When flowers and buds are dry, secure with a little fine fuse wire.

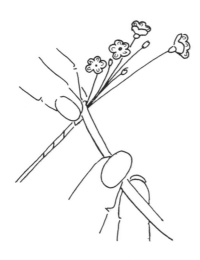

8 Using a little florist tape ¼ gauge, neatly tape spray together.

Use cutter no. A17 and A18 for leaves.

9 Finished spray.

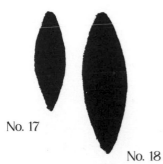

No. 17

No. 18

Note: The largest cutter in the set may be used for either a red petal or a leaf. Poinsettias come in red, pinks and a soft yellow.

1 To make the centres, roll a small piece of green paste (smaller than a pea) into a ball and then into a tear-drop shape. Insert a fine taped wire into centre.

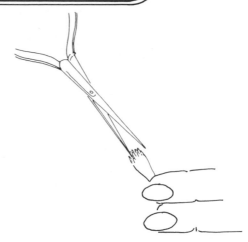

2 With small sharp scissors, make numerous incisions into the paste, causing it to appear like a mass of stamens.

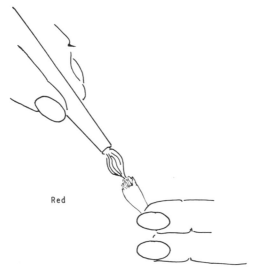

Red

3 Using red food colouring paint these 'stamens' red.

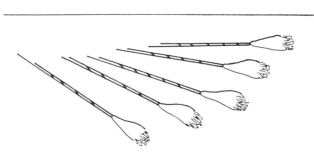

4 You will need about seven centres for a flower. (The actual flower has many more). Depending on the size of the flower you are making, increase the number of centres. Be sure to make an uneven number.

5 Use a minute bit of yellow paste about 1 mm in diameter, or less. Roll this into a tiny ball. Use Tool 4B to make an indentation into it, forming what appear to be 'lips'.

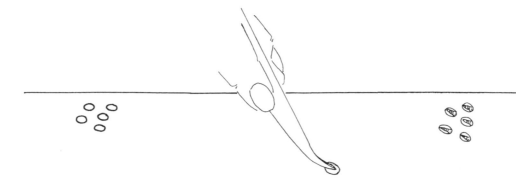

6 Brush on a tiny amount of gum glue to join 'lips' to green part of each centre. Leave to dry.

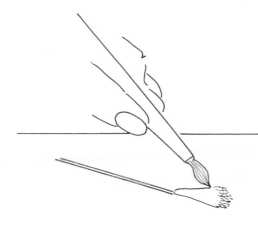

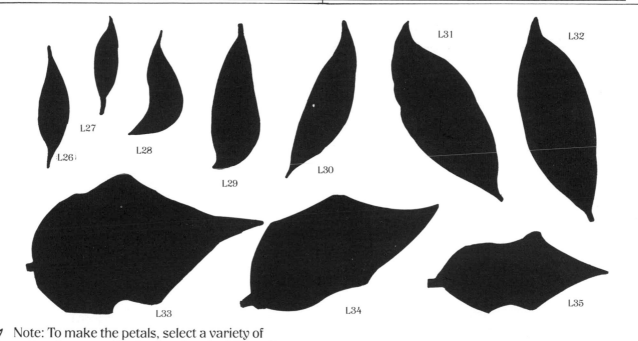

L26 L27 L28 L29 L30 L31 L32

L33 L34 L35

7 Note: To make the petals, select a variety of cutters from small to large using the L5 set. Cut out two or three of each size petal.

Bottom

8 Use fine fuse wire which has been covered in ¼ width green tape. Bend wires to angle suitable to hold petals. You will need to make between fifteen and twenty wires for each flower.

9 Mark in veins on each petal using a hibiscus petal veiner.

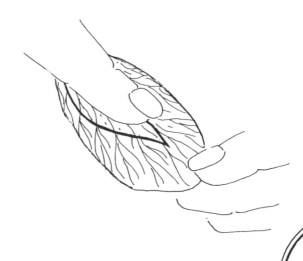

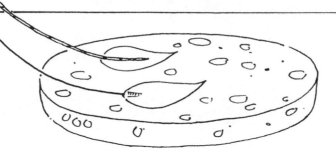

10 Rest petals upside down on foam. Attach wire, which has had gum glue brushed on to it, to each petal. Alternatively, roll out paste leaving a thicker base for the insertion of wire into each petal.

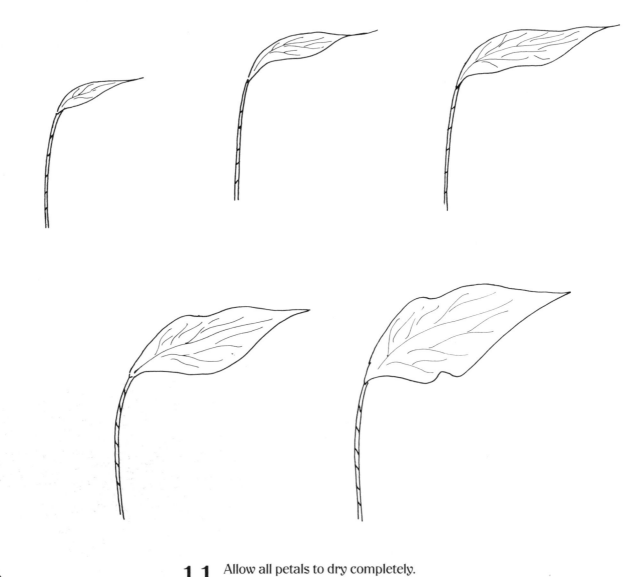

11 Allow all petals to dry completely.

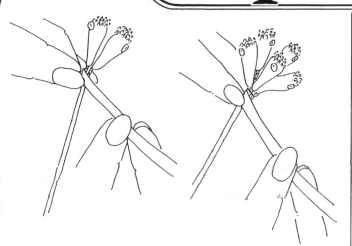

12 Begin assembling the flower by taping the centres together. Begin taping from the top of the wire and work down the stem.

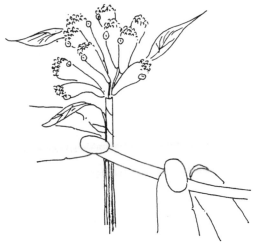

13 Now add small petals, ensuring that you do not make the flower symmetrical in the placing of the petals.

14 Continue to add petals, using the medium size petals.

16 Finished flower.

15 Finally add the large petals, again making sure the flower is not symmetrical. Cut off surplus stems with wire cutters.

*S*nowdrop

B
12

B
21

1 Using either Cutter No. B12 or B21 and white
   paste, cut out two shapes the same size.

2 Using tool 1A, place petals on soft foam. Gently
   work petals causing them to form a cup shape. Do
this to both petals.

3 Now using egg white or gum glue, carefully apply
   a little in the centre of one layer of petals.

4 Place the second layer of petals so that they lie
   between those of the first row.

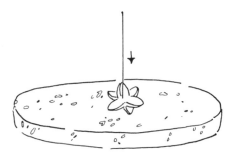

5 Cut off the tip of a stamen and gently ease the
   stamen through the centre of both rows of petals.

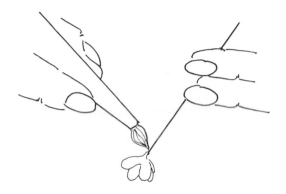

6 Lift up flower and carefully apply a little gum glue to the back of petals to secure to stamen.

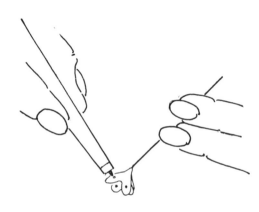

7 When dry, use a food colour pen or petal dust mixed with a little gin and carefully mark each petal with a green dot. A cocktail stick is preferable to a paint brush for this purpose.

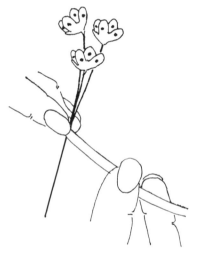

8 Make several flowers, and, when dry, tape together. A little fine fuse wire will help give the spray strength. The spray may be wired before being taped.

9 A spray.

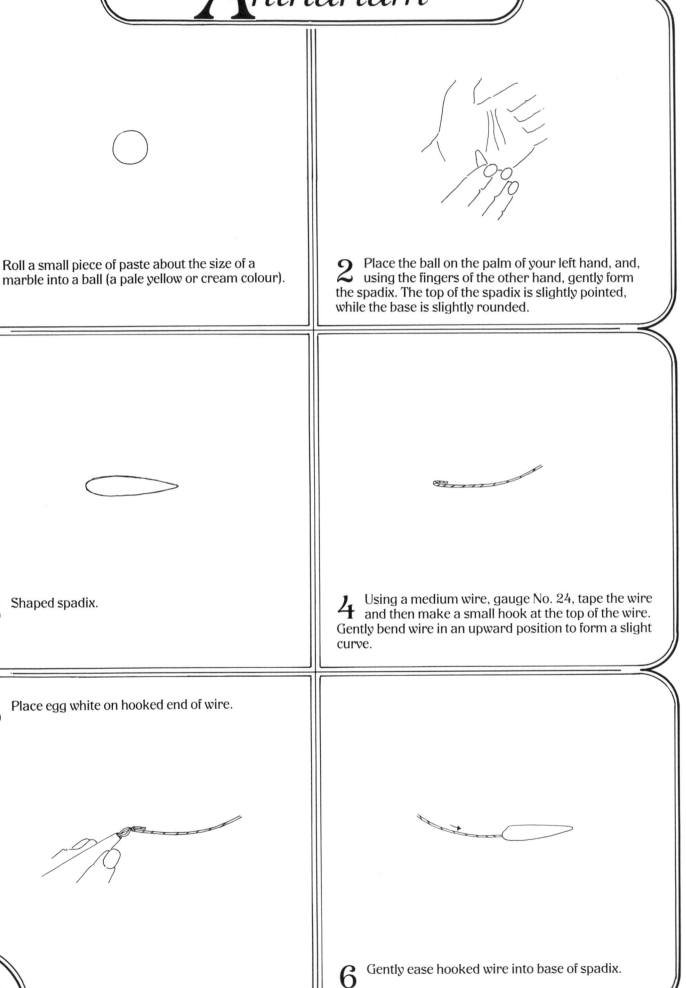

1 Roll a small piece of paste about the size of a marble into a ball (a pale yellow or cream colour).

2 Place the ball on the palm of your left hand, and, using the fingers of the other hand, gently form the spadix. The top of the spadix is slightly pointed, while the base is slightly rounded.

3 Shaped spadix.

4 Using a medium wire, gauge No. 24, tape the wire and then make a small hook at the top of the wire. Gently bend wire in an upward position to form a slight curve.

5 Place egg white on hooked end of wire.

6 Gently ease hooked wire into base of spadix.

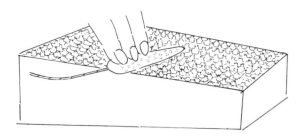

7 Using a grater (the fine rough side), gently roll the spadix over the grater allowing the impression to appear on the spadix.

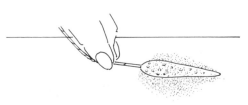

8 Place a little pollen on your worktop surface (either fine gelatin or maize meal mixed together with yellow or white chalk).

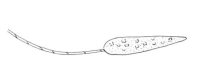

9 The complete spadix.

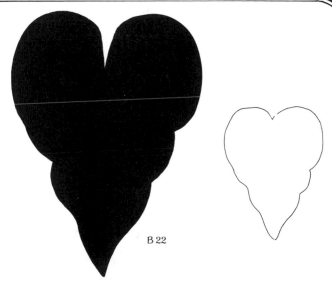

B 22

10 Roll out paste in colour of your choice (red, orange, pink, cream) on lightly greased surface. Cut out spathe using Cutter No. B22.

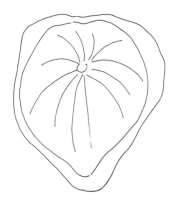

11 Mould of Anthurium made out of Plaster of Paris. The spathe of a real flower gives excellent results.

12 Place spathe over mould and evenly press petal over impression to form shape.

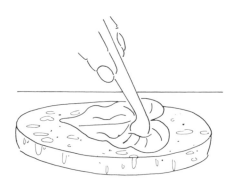

13 If you do not have a mould, shape the petal on a piece of fine foam. You may even wish to enhance the shape from the mould on the foam. Use tool No. 3A and 3B.

14 Place gum glue at the base of spadix. A third of the way down the spathe gently ease the spadix through petal.

15 Prop up with 'cloud' and leave to dry.

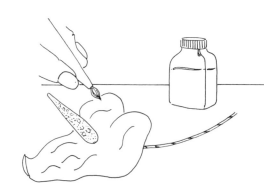

16 When flower is completely dry, paint with decorator's varnish. You may find that several coats are needed to give this flower the shiny finish it should have. A cooking spray may also be used.

17 Finished flower.

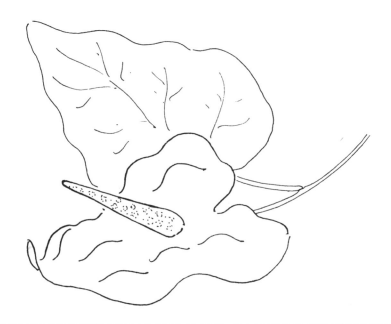

Bouvardia

Note: The same principle applies to the making of Daphne and Lilac.

1 Roll a small piece of paste into ball.

2 Shape into 'Mexican hat' – flat base and pointed tip.

B
71

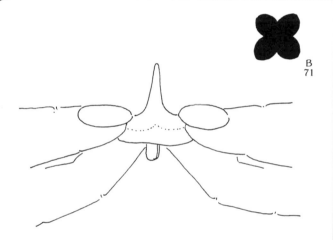

3 Using cutter No. B71, hold in left hand. Place icing paste on top of cutter and gently press paste over edge of cutter, causing flower to be cut out. Separate paste from cutter. Place surplus paste back into plastic bag.

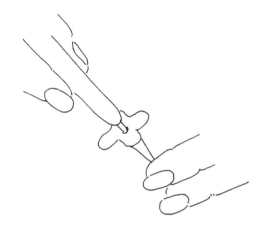

4 Using Tool No. 2A, place in centre of petals and begin working centre of flower, slightly hollowing it out. Petals should be level with each other and centre only slightly enlarged.

5 Using Tool No. 4A carefully work petal on petal pad ensuring petals are thin.

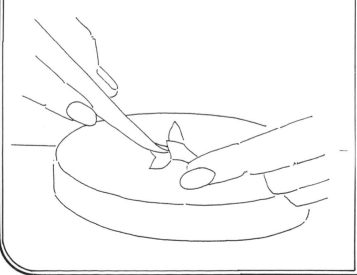

6 Gently pinch petals together creating a slight point on the edge of the petal. Trumpet part of flower should be as narrow as possible.

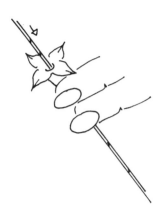

7 Using a soft wire which has been taped, gently ease down the throat of the flower until it is not visible.

8 Finished flower with stem not showing in throat of flower.

9 To make a bud, use a small piece of paste and shape into tear drop.

10 Using same gauge wire as for flower, dip into 'glue' and ease on bud.

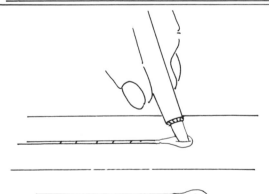

11 Take a sharp knife and carefully cut paste to form four petals.
Shade buds and back of flowers with a pale pink petal dust.

12 A spray.

Briar Rose

Note: The buds are the same as ordinary rose buds.

1 Roll cotton around finger 30x to form loops. Secure with fine fuse wire on both sides of the loop. Cut through centre to make two.

2 Tape a firm wire (gauge No. 24) in green.

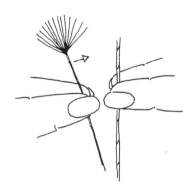

3 Join cotton to main stem with florist tape. Evenly space cotton stamens around centre.

4 Cotton joined to stem.

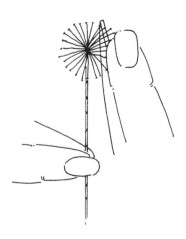

5 Using a small pair of scissors or a sharp knife, frill edges of cotton.

6 Top view of finished cotton centre with frilled edges to which a tiny paste centre has been added.

7 Dip the tip of the cotton stamens into white vegetable fat.

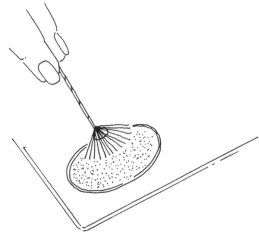

8 Now place the stamen tips into coloured 'pollen', maize meal or gelatin.

Note: Make all the centres you will need before beginning the petals.

No. 27

9 Using Cutter No. 27, cut out five petals. Cover with thin plastic whilst working one petal at a time. Alternatively use an Easy Rose Cutter and cut out all the petals at once.

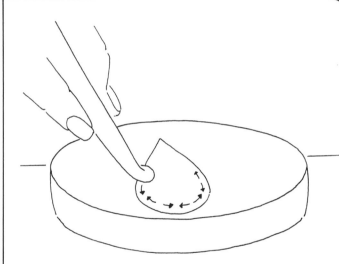

10 Using Tool 3A or 6A work the edges of the petals on the petal pad ensuring petals are very thin and slightly frilled.

12 Allow petals to rest on convex formers until they are holding their shape, but not dry. Note, the curled part of the petal is facing upwards.

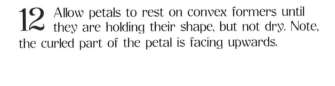

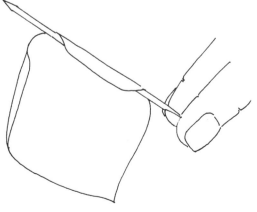

11 Using a cocktail stick curl petals backwards towards the dry side of the petal.

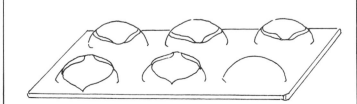

Briar Rose

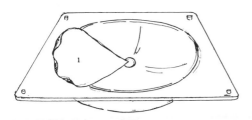

13 Using appropriate petal former 1A or 2A, depending on size of flower, lightly grease with a little white vegetable fat.

Take a very tiny piece of paste and flatten to form a tiny base on which to secure petals.

Using egg white or gum glue, place petals into former.

Note: The 'curl' in the Briar Rose petals may curl facing in towards the centre, or it may curl backwards giving the flower an almost flat appearance.

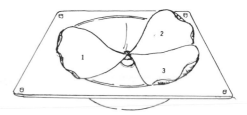

14 Add second and third petals.

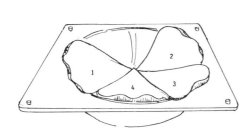

15 Add fourth petal.

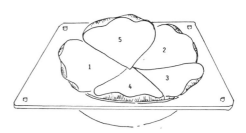

16 Finally add the fifth petal.

18 Finished flower.

Note: The calyx for this flower could have been added into the flower at Step 13 if a flat finish was needed, or it can be placed on to the dry flower and curl backwards away from the petals. See instruction on Page 138.

17 Place a little gum glue in the centre of the petals and carefully ease the stamens into the centre of the flower.

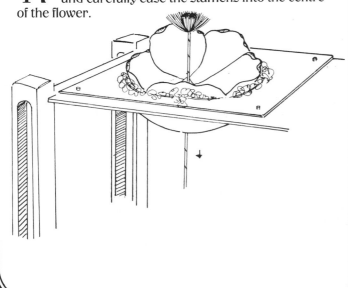

Briar Rose

JEM - Easy Rose Cutters

These cutters are ideal for the Briar Rose, or quick roses and any other flower which has five petals. When using these cutters to make a Briar Rose, leave the centre of the paste thicker than the petals. This will add strength to the flower enabling it to support the stamen stem. Work petals on a petal pad and curl as required.

50mm

60mm

90mm

100mm

80mm

110mm

Carnation

1 Roll paste in a colour of your choice into a tear-drop shape. The base should be about the size of a small pea, with the wider part flat.

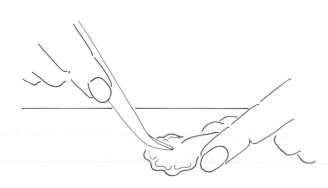

2 Flatten the wider side of paste with fingers, and then use Tool 4A to frill the paste.

3 Pick up the petal and fold frilled edges backwards and forwards as if creating a fan.

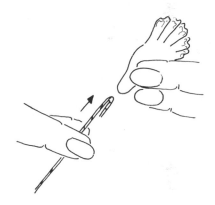

4 Using a taped wire (gauge 26), gently ease into base of petal. Remember to place a little egg white on the wire first to ensure that the paste does not come off the wire.

5 Place petal in upright position by sticking wire into either polystyrene or florist's oasis which you have previously covered with tin foil to prevent 'fluff' getting into your icing. Insert two fine white stamens into centre, level with the petals.

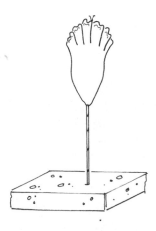

6 Roll out paste fairly thinly and cut out Carnation petal, using Cutter No B41.

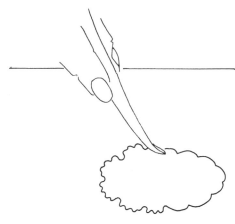

7 Using Tool No 4A or 2B, gently flute all the scallops, allowing the edges to crack if they tend to do so.

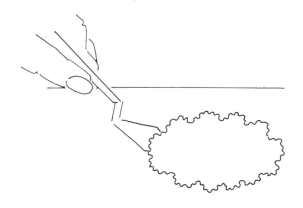

8 Using a small artist's palette or Tool 8B, pick up the petal.

9 Fold the petal in half.

10 Fold in half again – creating four layers of petal.

11 Using a paint brush, apply gum glue to open edges of petal.

12 Attach it to centre. Make sure that when you join this petal to the centre it is level with the original petal. Do not allow it to slip below the centre height. Continue to add petals in the same way until you feel you have sufficient petals for your carnation. It is not a good idea to make it too heavy.

Note: This is all that is required if you wish to make a feathered carnation for a bouquet. When completely dry, cover base with ½ width florist tape.

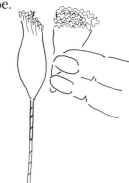

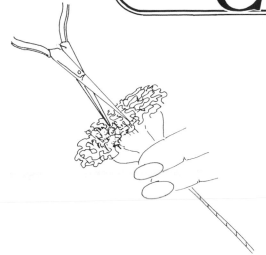

13 Using a small pair of sharp scissors, cut into the petals – encouraging them to fan out and away from each other.

B38

14 To make the calyx, use cutter No B38 and dull green paste which has not been rolled out too thinly.

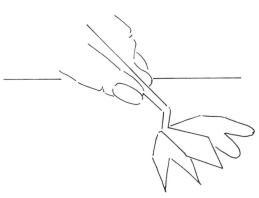

15 Using artist's palette-knife, flatten each sepal, causing the pointed tip to become slightly rounded.

16 a. Brush a little gum glue on the base of the calyx and attach it to the carnation.
b. Now cut out calyx with Cutter No B55. Add a touch of gum glue to the centre only.
c. Attach this tiny calyx to the previous one, allowing the sepals to stand free.

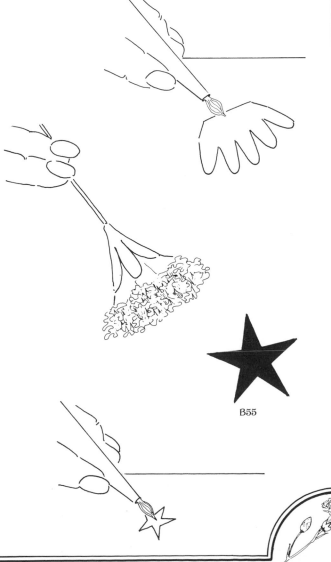

B55

17 Finished carnation.

1 To make the column, tape a piece of fine fuse wire. Cover the tip with a little paste and mould this into the correct shape. Use a fine paint brush, or a cocktail stick and food colouring, to paint in the markings.

2 Cut out the lip, using Cutter No 26. Lightly flute the front of the petal, using Tool 4A, or 2B.

No 26

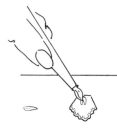

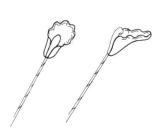

3 Roll out a tiny piece of paste into a sausage. Use a sharp craft knife and split the sausage in half. Place this on the back of the lip in the centre. Lightly brush with gum glue and apply a little yellow pollen (maize meal) to this.

4 Place the column in the lip. If necessary, use a little gum glue to secure the sides of the lip to the column.

B17

5 Cut out the lateral sepals, using Cutter No B17.

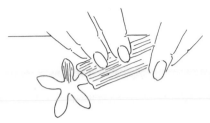

6 Use a corn leaf veiner and mark each sepal.

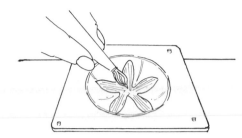

7 Place a little gum glue in the centre of the sepals, which should be supported in Flower Support No. 2A.

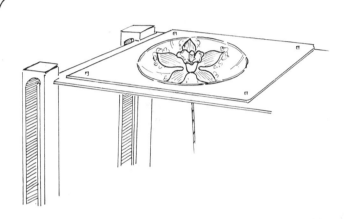

8 Place the support in the Handy Holder and ease lip into sepals. The lip should be in front of the lateral sepal and have two sepals evenly arranged on either side of the lip. Support the flower with a little 'cloud' if necessary. Allow flower to dry completely.

Note: To make a half open orchid, assemble as above and allow flower to hang upside down to dry over the side of the Handy Holder.

9 A spray of baby orchids.

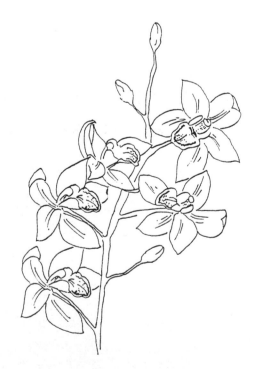

Daffodil

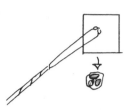

1 Tape a fairly firm wire, gauge 24. Cover top with yellow paste. Using tips of fingers, create three flat sides to centre of top of pistil.

2 Roll out paste into fine strips and attach to pistil using gum glue, if necessary. If pistil is not dry, you will find that the paste stamens will simply meld into the paste on the wire. Alternatively use firm headless stamens emerged in vegetable fat which has been coloured yellow to match pistil. Tape.

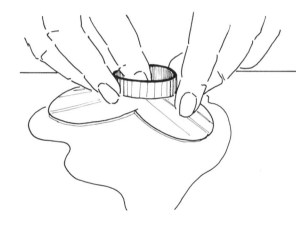

B25

3 Roll out paste on a board lightly spread with white vegetable fat.
Using Cutter B25 cut one.
Lift all left over paste and return it to a plastic bag to prevent drying.

4 Using Tool No 4A or 2B, flute edges of sepals.

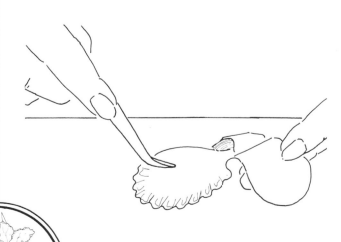

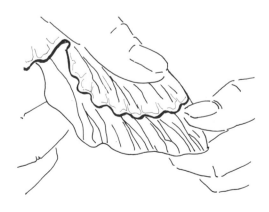

5 Press sepals against orchid veiner to create veined impression on sepals. Place on petal former 5A.

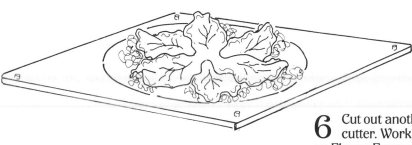

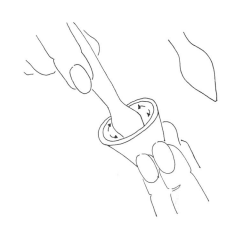

6 Cut out another row of sepals using the same cutter. Work as before. Place second row of sepals on Flower Former 5A, allowing the second row to fall between the petals of the first row. Use a little 'cloud' to lift petals upwards.

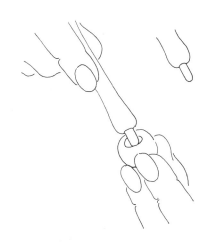

7 Roll a small amount of paste about the size of a marble into a 'ball'.
Using Tool No 2A, push into centre of ball and begin to shape centre by rotating tool slightly.

8 Now using Tool No 2B, press tool into centre of ball and rotate tool, increasing size of centre of trumpet, forming a 'cup'.

10 By rotating the paste by lifting it up and at the same time causing the edges of the 'cup' to frill, continue to work 'cup' until it is evenly frilled.

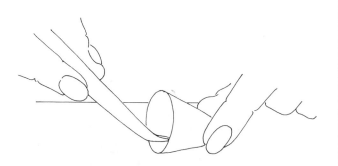

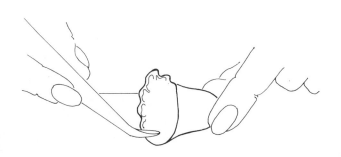

9 Using Tool 4A, place 'cup' on worktop surface, which is lightly greased, and begin working the 'cup'.

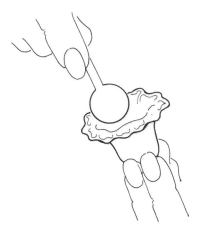

11 Using Tool 6A, hollow out centre of trumpet and ensure that edges of trumpet are bending slightly outwards.
Using petal dust, shade fluted edge of trumpet with darker colour before attaching to sepals, if desired..

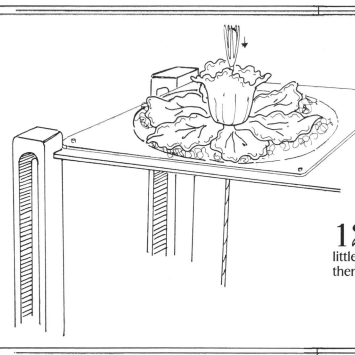

No. 52

12 Paint a little gum glue on the centre of the sepals and place the trumpet in position. Use a little more gum glue in the centre of the trumpet and then gently ease the pistil into the flower.

13 When flower is dry, bend flower over using a small pair of pliers. Using some straw coloured paste yellow/beige and cutter No. 52 cut out the 'dry' calyx for this flower.
Vein with orchid veiner, or corn leaf veiner and twist petal around the bent stem slightly standing away from the stem.

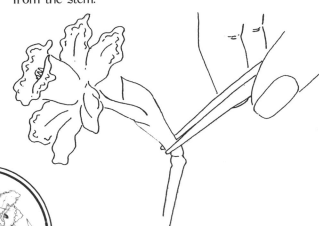

14 Completed flower.

$\mathcal{F}$rangipani

No 48

1 Using Cutter No 48, cut out five petals in white paste. Cover with soft plastic or a plastic lid to prevent drying out.

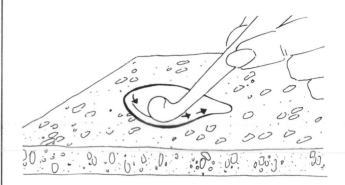

2 Place one petal at a time on foam. Use Tool 3B, gently easing tool down left hand side of petal. Begin at the centre of the top of the petal and end just before the petal tapers off.

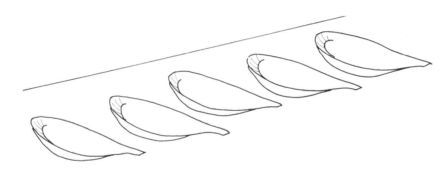

3 Lift petal off foam and place on worktop surface in order of production. Ensure that left hand side is curving inwards and the rest of the petal is resting flat on worktop surface.

Note: Do not attempt to assemble this flower until petals are holding the curved shape. However, do not forget to watch petals, as petals which are too dry will simply crack when trying to assemble them. It is a good idea to make enough petals for two or three flowers, depending on climatic conditions, before attempting to assemble the flower.

4 When petals are still soft but holding their shape, using egg white or gum glue, carefully place glue on right hand side of petal, beginning just below the halfway mark on the petal to the base.

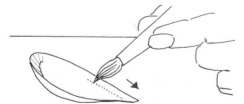

5 Line petals up in a row after each addition of glue. The important thing to remember here is to watch the top of the petals – keep them in a straight line.

Frangipani

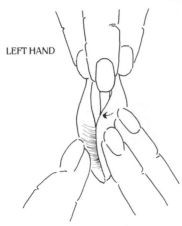

LEFT HAND

6 Now using your left hand, pick up the petals at the base and hang them downwards. Using your right hand, gently encourage the last petal in the line to join the back of the first petal.

7 Carefully twist petals away from yourself, causing them to hold together securely.

8 Place petals in Handy Holder in one of the small open holes and open up the petals carefully. Remember that the frangipani opens in many different stages. From the above steps you may make semi-open, half open and fully open flowers – depending on how far you open the petals once they are in the stand.

9 To stem this flower – allow flower to almost dry (petals not base) and then gently ease a fine, hooked, taped wire into the centre of the flower.

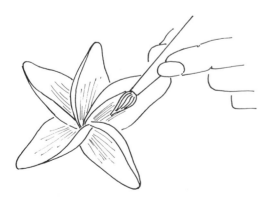

10 When flower is completely dry, using petal dust, shade petals yellow where indicated. The centre has a touch of orange in it.

11 Turn flower upside down, resting it on a piece of paper towel and shade back of petals as indicated in a soft pink/brown shade.

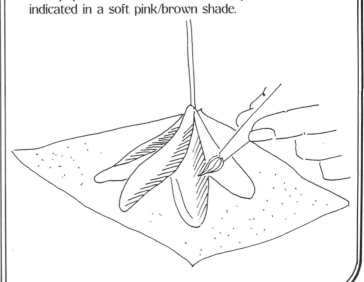

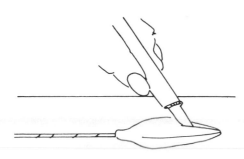

12 To make a bud, roll a ball of paste into a tear-drop shape just a bit smaller than the flower. Using a sharp knife, gently cut the five petals in a straight line.

13 Now twist the bud; the top half to your left and the base to the right – see illustration.

14 Insert taped wire.

15 Finished spray.

Baby Fuchsia

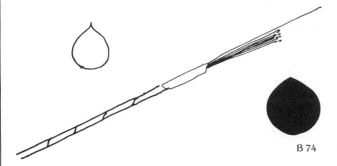

B 74

1 Using very fine fuse wire, join 9 fine stamens together (or less if not for show work). One stamen, the pistil, must be slightly higher than the others. Cover wire with tape.

Using cutter No. B74, cut one petal and gently ease over base of stamens to hide wire. This also gives you a base on which to stick the other petals.

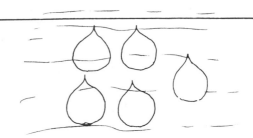

2 Roll out paste thinly and cut out four more petals using Cutter B74 or B75. Cover with thin plastic, or a plastic lid, to prevent drying too rapidly.

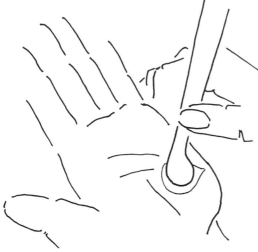

3 Place petals in the palm of your hand and, with Tool No. 3B, gently work edges of petals.

4 Using gum glue to secure, add petals to stamens, allowing each additional petal to slightly overlap the last petal.

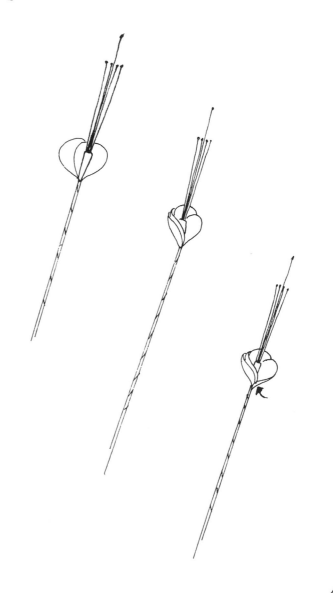

5 With cutter No. B73, cut out calyx in a contrasting colour.

B 73

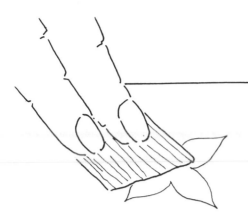

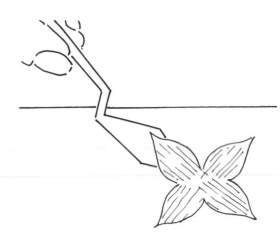

6 Using a corn leaf veiner, mark sepals.

7 Carefully pick up calyx with an artist's palette knife.

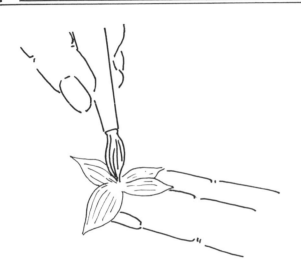

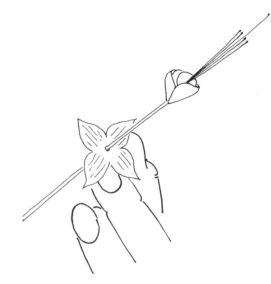

8 Place a small amount of egg white or gum glue in the centre of the calyx with the veined side uppermost.

9 Ease calyx on to stem.

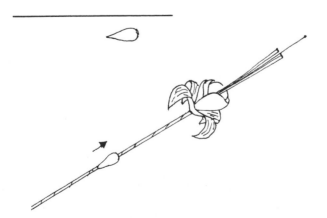

Note: It is interesting to note that the shading of the stamens and the calyx in this flower are usually the same colour.

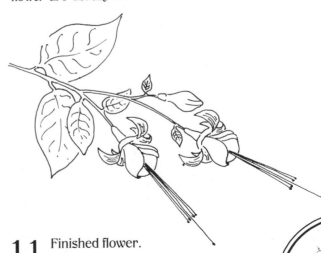

10 Curl Sepal backwards.
Take a tiny piece of green paste formed into a small tear drop and ease up the stem of the flower to form the seedbox of the flower, neatening the calyx.

11 Finished flower.

Baby Fuchsia

Hyacinth

B 57

1 Roll a small piece of paste into a ball between the
size of a pea and a marble.
Flatten outside edges of the ball, creating a point in the
centre, forming what looks like a Mexican hat.
Using cutter B57, hold this in your hand and place
Mexican hat over cutter, ensuring that the centre of the
'hat' is over the centre of the shape.

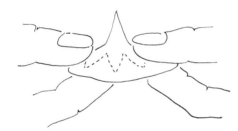

2 Gently press fingers over edges of cutter, causing
flower to form.

3 Using Tool No 2B, form throat in flower.

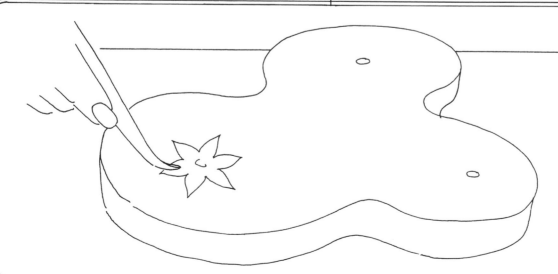

4 Place trumpet part of flower in Mexican Petal Pad
and using Tool 4A thin petals evenly.

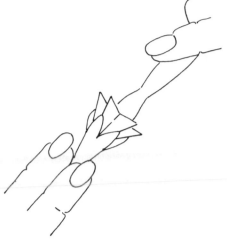

5 Use Tool No 8A or Tool 9B to vein inside petals.

6 Pinch outside edges of petals together and slightly tilt backwards.

7 Using a fine fuse wire which has been taped and tightly hooked, gently ease stem into flower, causing the wire to disappear into the base of the flower.

8 Make a number of flowers and then tape them together, forming a spray suitable to use in a cluster arrangement or bouquet.

Note: This flower grows in a cluster on a single stem with the flowers appearing on all sides of the stem.

*J*asmine

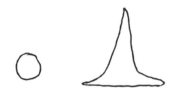

1 Using a small piece of paste about the size of a pea or smaller, form a ball.
Flatten the edges of the ball forming a pointed centre like a Mexican hat.

B60

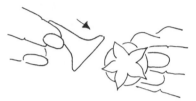

2 Now holding Cutter No B60 in your hand, place the centre of the Mexican hat over the centre of the cutter.

3 Press fingers over edge of cutter, causing flower to be cut out.

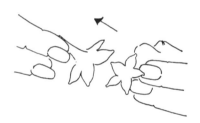

4 Gently ease the paste off the cutter forming the jasmine. Return surplus paste to plastic bag.

5 Hold flower upside-down on the palm of your hand. Using Tool 4A, work edges of petals until thin.

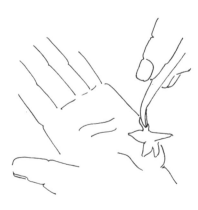

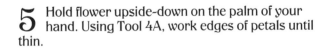

6 Now using Tool 2A, gently insert the point into the centre, making sure not to increase the size of the hole formed.

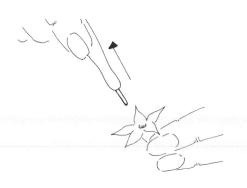

7 Remove Tool 2A, ensuring that the hole formed is small, and that the petals are level with each other.

8 Now using fingers, first flatten petals and then lightly pinch a few of them and allow them to curl backwards.

Note: It is interesting to note that jasmine petals are very thin and very uneven in appearance as they tend to curl in any direction. Some petals are pointed, while others appear to be slightly rounded.

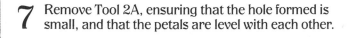

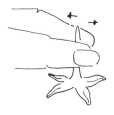

9 Hold flower upside-down and gently twist stem this way and that, causing the trumpet to become thin and narrow. Break off excess paste.

10 Using covered fine fuse wire gently push through centre of the flower allowing it to just show at the top of the flower.

12 Roll a tiny amount of paste on a stamen.

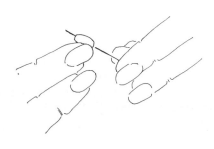

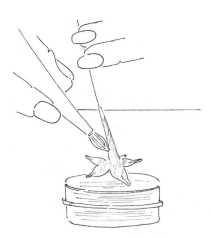

11 Hold flower upside down over pale mauve/pink petal dust and shade back of petal.

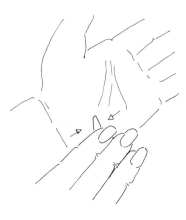

13 Roll paste on stamen in the palm of your hand to form bud.

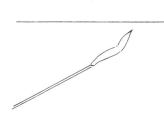

14 Finished Bud.

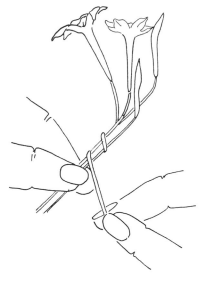

15 Join buds, leaves and flowers into a spray using florist tape to secure.

16 Jasmine spray.

Note: Make several flowers, buds and also leaves, using cutters Nos 17 and 18. Remember to vein leaves appropriately.

Marmalade Bush

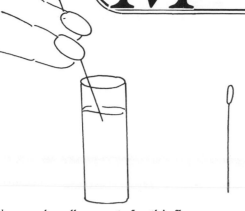

1 Use a pale yellow paste for this flower.

Tape a small piece of fine fuse wire, or simply use a stamen.

Dip the tip into some gum glue or egg white. Using the yellow paste, take a minute amount of paste and cover the tip.

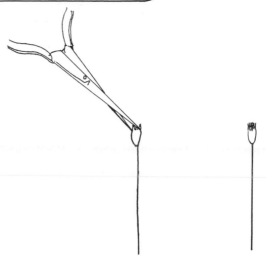

2 Using a pair of sharp scissors, make a number of incisions into the paste creating a feathery effect.

3 Now take a small piece of paste about the size of a pea and roll it into a ball.

Flatten the edges and leave the centre in a cone shape and form a Mexican hat.

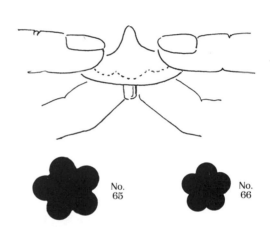

4 Using Cutter No. 65 or 66, place the paste over the cutter, ensuring that the centre of the Mexican hat is in the middle of the cutter. Gently ease fingers over the edge of the cutter, causing the flower to be formed.

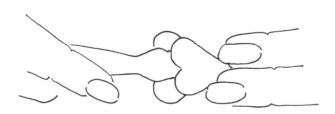

5 Using Tool 2A and 2B, begin to open the throat of the flower.

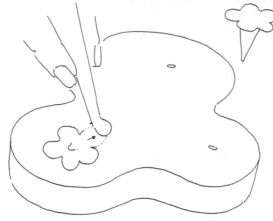

6 Now using Tool 4A, begin to work the edges of the petals. It is important to remember that three petals on each flower are slightly larger than the remaining two petals. Work petals on a Mexican petal pad.

7 When petals and throat have been worked sufficiently, place a little gum glue or egg white into throat of flower and carefully ease the centre of the flower into position.

The stamens should be almost level with the top of the petals.

8 When flower is finished, shade it with darker yellow and orange petal dust. Some flowers on a spray are mostly yellow and some mostly orange. A good mixture of both colours is required to form a spray.

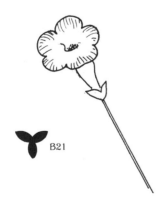

B21

9 Cutter B21 should be used as a calyx for this flower.

10 Using cutter No. 16, make a number of small leaves to attach to spray. Tape together.

No 16

Equipment

A summary of the equipment used in the making of the flowers is given below:

* A selection of cutters from the JEM range.

* JEM Tools

* JEM Handy Holder and Flower Supports

* JEM Tape cutter

* JEM Petal Pad & Mexican Petal Pad

* JEM veiners – a variety

* Florist tape – green, white and brown

* Florist wire

* Fuse wire

* Petal dust

* Paste food colouring

* Plastic roller

* Laminate worktop surface

* Artist's palette knives

* Artist's plastic palette tray

* Paint brushes – good quality – different sizes

* Sponge-foam

* Stamens

* Cotton thread

* Duvet stuffing 'cloud'

* Craft knife

* Medical tweezers

* Small scissors

* Wire cutters

* Pliers

* Cocktail sticks

* Tylose C1000p

Narcissus

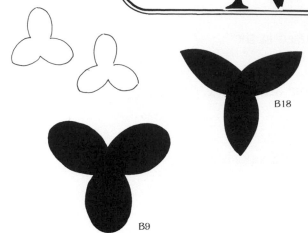

1 Using Cutter No. B9 or B18, depending on the particular flower you wish to make, roll out paste and cut two. Place sepals under soft plastic to prevent drying out.

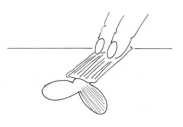

2 Use a corn leaf veiner. Press in the veins from the centre to the outside edge of sepals.

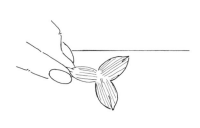

3 Gently crease sepals between fingers to create a slight ridge effect on the petals.

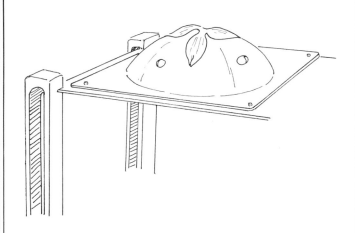

4 Place on flower former 1A upside-down. (Convex position.)

5 Work the second row of sepals in the same way, then using egg white to secure, place the top row of sepals between the first row of sepals.

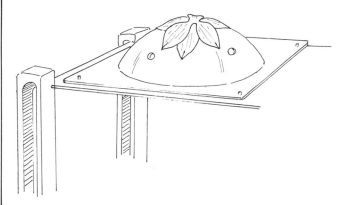

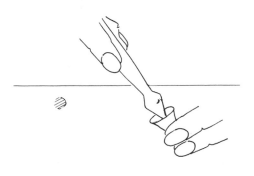

6 Use a deeper shade of paste. Roll a ball about the size of a pea. Using Tool No. 2B, begin to open throat of flower.

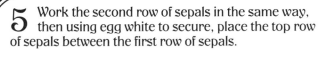

7 Now using Tool No. 4A, gently flute outside edges of centre of petal, ensuring that the inside of the throat is evenly worked and thin.

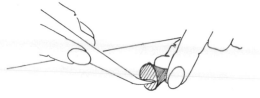

Note: An easy way to create a frilled effect is to press your tool into the paste, then quickly lift it up. Continue to press tool against the last impression overlapping the indentation marks.

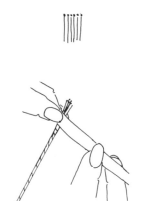

8 Using six fine stamens, cut them to fit into the throat so they are just below the fluted lip. Join to florist wire, previously taped. Tape to secure.

9 Now gently ease stamens into position through the 'cup' of the flower.

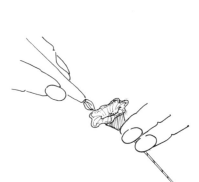

10 The tip of the frill may be shaded if desired.

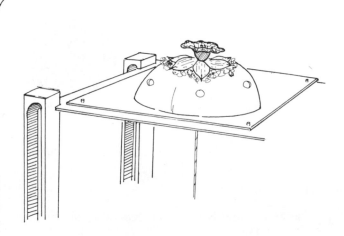

11 Apply egg white or gum glue to centre of sepals. Ease stem of cup through centre. Prop up sepals with a little 'cloud' if necessary.

12 A finished flower.

Pansy

Note: Unless you are very artistic, it is recommended that you use yellow paste for this flower and shade the flower with either a dark brown colouring or black.

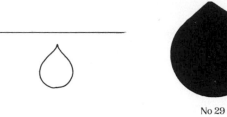

No 29

1 Using Cutter No 29 or 30, roll out paste and cut out four petals, covering petals with soft plastic to prevent drying.

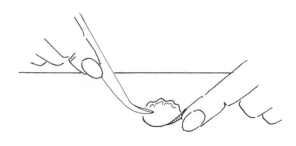

2 Use Tool No 4A or 2B to work the edges of the petals, causing them to frill.

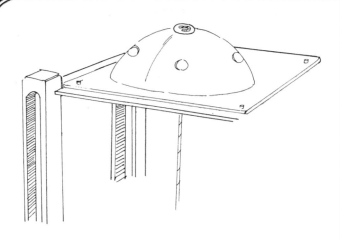

3 Place flower support No 1A in the convex position in the handy holder, lightly cover the support with a little white vegetable fat and place a small flat piece of paste over the centre. Ease a fine taped, flat hooked wire into the paste. Apply egg white to centre.

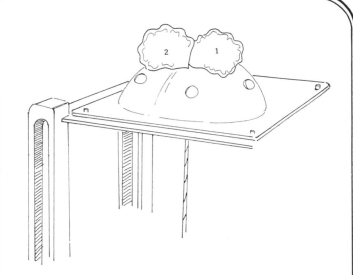

4 Now begin adding frilled petals. The first petal is placed on the right hand side; the second petal slightly overlaps the base of the first petal.

5 Add the third petal on the right hand side, and the fourth petal on the left hand side.

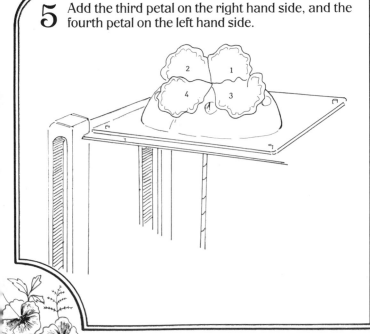

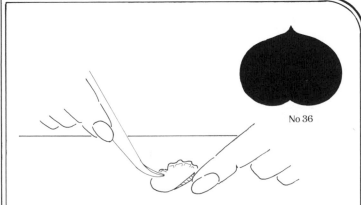

No 36

6 Now use Cutter No 36, and, depending on whether you used Cutter No 29 or 30, you will either roll out the paste thinly or thickly to increase the size of the petal whilst working it.
Begin working paste with Tool No 4A to increase the size of the 'skirt'. Finally flute edges with Tool No 2B or 4A.

74

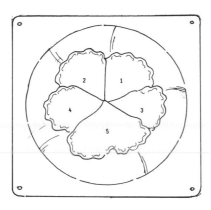

7 Place petal on support. The 'skirt' overlaps the side petals.

8 Take a minute piece of either green paste or a deeper yellow. Make a tiny ball about 1 mm in diameter. Place this over the centre of flower. Use a little egg white to secure.
Using Tool No 4A, press the point into the centre, causing the sides to lift up slightly. The sides may be touched up with a little egg white and a little yellow pollen. Leave to dry completely.

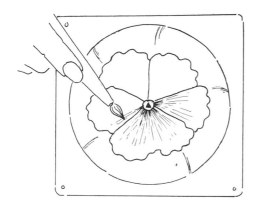

9 When the flower is completely dry, carefully shade the lower two petals and skirt with non-toxic water colours. Place one or two drops of dishwashing liquid into a small jar of water – this helps to remove any vegetable fat from the surface of petals, helping the paint to be applied evenly.

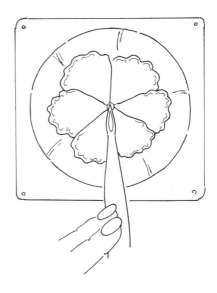

11 Place calyx on foam, and, using tool No 3B, ease tool over sepal towards centre of calyx. This will cause sepals to curl inwards.

No 74

10 Using Cutter No 74, cut out the calyx in green paste.

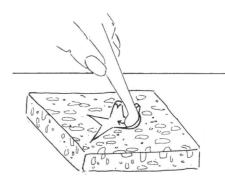

Pansy

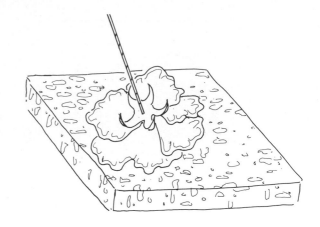

12 Pick up the calyx, and, using a little egg white in the centre of the calyx, attach it to the flower, ensuring that the sepals of the calyx turn away from the flower. Pinch individual sepals together so the tips look joined.

13 Turn flower upside-down, resting on foam, to allow calyx to dry.

14 Finished pansy.

Poppy

Note: If you have real poppies, or coloured illustrations, follow the natural colours as far as possible.

1 Use a fairly strong wire if you plan to make a life-size poppy. (Gauge 24). Tape it with green tape and make a tight hook at the top of the wire.

2 Use some dull green paste to cover the hook, forming a cone shape – the rounded part at the top of the wire.

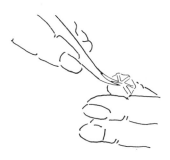

3 Use some sharp tweezers and pinch the top of the centre, forming what looks like a flower with seven divisions.

4 Carefully place a little gum glue over the raised bits of the pistil and dip into yellow pollen (i.e. coloured maize meal).

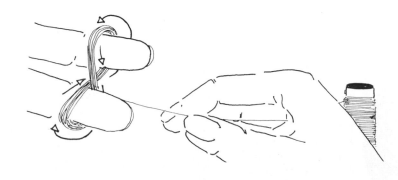

5 Now take some yellow cotton. Twist the cotton around your index and middle fingers in a figure of 8.

Poppy

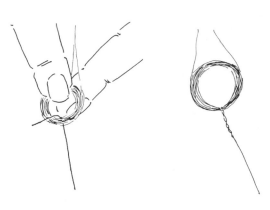

6 Remove from fingers, and, using some fine fuse wire, tightly grip the cotton by twisting the wire firmly into the base of the cotton circle.

7 You will need to make about three cotton rings, depending on how many stamens you wish the poppy to have. In reality they have many stamens. Place the cotton rings evenly around the centre you have made.

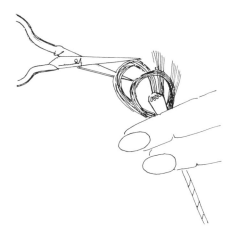

8 Slit the cotton with small sharp scissors and spread the cotton out evenly around the middle. Trim the stamens.

9 Lightly tip the cotton tips in white vegetable fat and then dip them into the pollen. Use a pin to remove the surplus pollen from the cotton and to separate those bits which stick together.

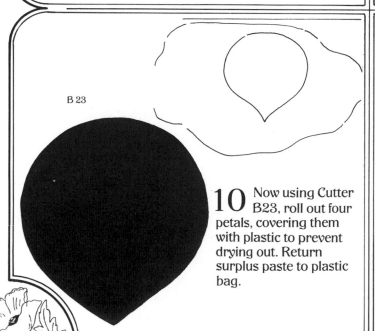

B 23

10 Now using Cutter B23, roll out four petals, covering them with plastic to prevent drying out. Return surplus paste to plastic bag.

11 Using Tool 2B or 4A, flute the edges of the petal ensuring that the edges are very frilly.

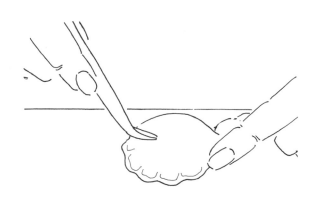

12 Vein petal using a reinforced maize leaf, or corn leaf vein by firmly pressing against paste petal resting in the palm of your hand.

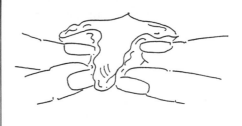

13 Now pinch the petals between your fingers causing the petal to actually crease. Place petal over a convex shape to partially dry. Flower former 2A is a good size, or a ping pong ball, cut in half.

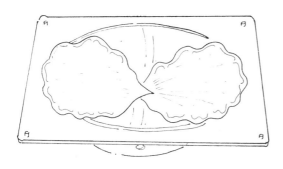

14 Using flower former 1A, place petals in position. The second petal will be directly opposite the first, slightly overlapping the first petal. Use gum glue to secure each petal.

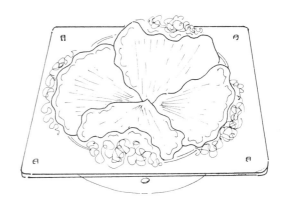

15 The third petal will be between the first two petals. The fourth petal will be directly opposite the third petal, slightly overlapping the base of the third petal.

16 Place a little gum glue in the centre of the petals and gently ease the centre of the flower into position. Petals may be propped up with 'cloud' if necessary.

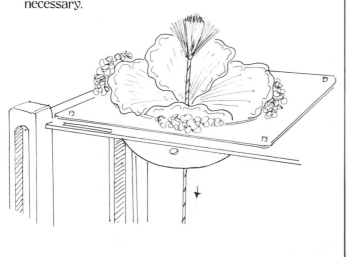

17 The finished flower.

Primula

Note: Two shades are needed for this flower.

No. 13

No. 15

1 Using Cutter No. 13, cut out one petal in the lighter shade.

2 Now using the darker shade, or yellow paste, cut the centre of the flower out using Cutter No. 15.

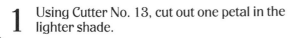

3 Place the smaller flower into the centre of the bigger flower, and using a Tool No. 3A, work the two flowers into each other making sure you do not break either flower. Work on a petal pad.

4 Push stamen or very fine, taped fuse wire, through centre of the flower.

5 Now take a tiny piece of green paste and make the calyx of the flower. Shape it into a tiny cone with a flat top. Ease the calyx up the stem, using a bit of egg white on the flat top to ensure it sticks to the flower.

6 Make many flowers and form into a posy by taping together.

Tulip

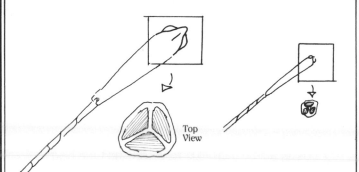
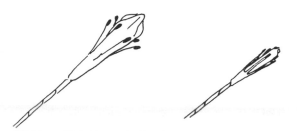

1 Tape a firm wire, gauge 24. Using yellow paste, roll a sausage about 2 cm long to fit on the end of the wire. Do not make this too heavy. Using the tips of your fingers shape the top into three even sections which will create a three-sided pistil. Illustration has been increased in size to indicate flat side of pistil.

2 You may either make the stamens out of black paste by simply rolling the paste into long thin sausages ± 1½ cm long, or by simply cutting six black stamens and pressing into the pistil before it dries. Illustration has been increased in size.

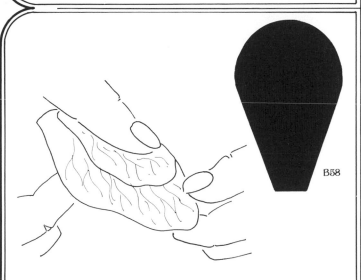

3 Using Cutter B58, cut out six petals. Cover with plastic to prevent drying. Press petals against orchid veiner to vein.

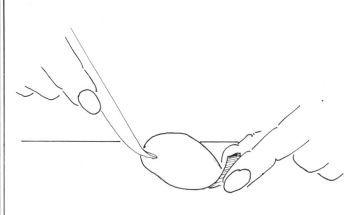

4 Using Tool No 4A or 2B, gently flute edges. The tops of the petals are slightly more frilled than the sides.

5 Place petals over artist's palette to partially dry. Give each petal a slight crease down the centre to enable it to form a 'cup like' effect when the petals are joined together.

6 Using flower former No. 2A, space three petals in the base, ensuring that petals fit in evenly, and all cover the centre hole in the flower support. Use a little gum glue to secure.

Tulip

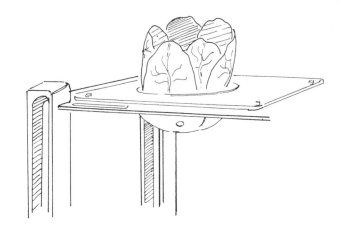

7 Using a little gum glue to secure, add the next three petals between the first row of petals, ensuring that the base of each petal rests over the centre hole of the flower former.

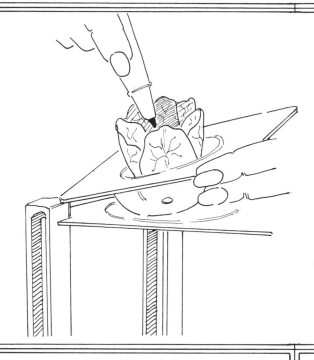

8 Using black food colouring, or a food colour pen, paint in markings at the base of flower. Dry.

9 Paint a little gum glue on to the base of the wired stamens and place in the centre of the petals. Dry.

10 When flower is dry, lightly shade the back of the flower with petal dust.

Water-lily

Note: The stamens of the water-lily are often the same shade as the petals, with a yellow tinge at the tips. Use petal dust for this effect.

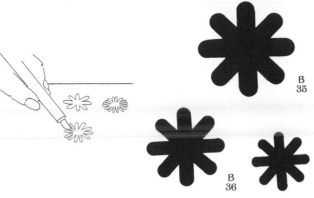

1 Cut two petals each, using Cutters No. B37, B36 and B35. Using a sharp knife, spilt each petal into two.

2 Place the six layers of petals one on top of the other, allowing the petals to fall in between each other. The largest petals at the base.

4 Using Cutter B34, cut two more layers. Pinch tips with fingers and attach holding stem upside down. Make sure centre forms what appears to be a tightly formed mass of stamens. When dry, dust tips yellow.

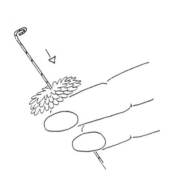

B34

3 Gently ease a 26 gauge taped, hooked wire through the layers of paste. Ensure the wire is hidden and the 'stamens' are forming a cup-like shape. Allow centre to hang down, or place in petal former 3A to cup.

5 Three shades of the same colour paste are needed for the petals. (See Shading of Paste for details on how to mix the shades). Begin with the largest cutter and the palest shade. Use Cutter No. 21 and cut out nine thin petals. Cover petals with soft plastic to prevent drying out.

No. 21

6 Using index finger and thumb, slightly fold outside edge of rounded end of petals together. Place petal on foam and gently pull Tool No. 4A down the centre of the petal causing the petal to 'cup' slightly.

7 Leave petals on work top surface to partially dry.

No. 20

8 Now use middle shade and Cutter No. 20. Repeat method, cutting out a further nine petals.

No. 19

9 Use darkest shade and smallest Cutter No. 19. Cut out the final nine petals. Repeat as before.

10 To assemble flower, place a small, flat piece of paste in the middle of flower support 1A.

11 Begin with the largest petals, allowing them to overlap. It will be necessary to use egg white or gum glue after each petal is placed to ensure that they stick together.

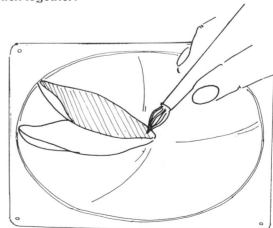

*W*ater - *lily*

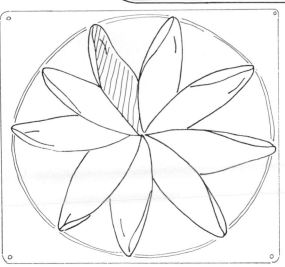

12 Completed first row of petals.

13 Now place the middle sized petals in position. These petals are placed between the outside petals.

14 Finally, add the small darker petals, using gum glue. Place them between the middle layer of petals as previously.

15 Place gum glue or egg white in the centre of the flower and then place stamens in position.

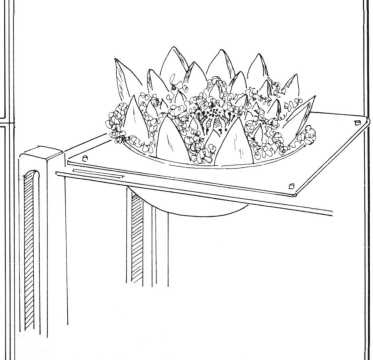

16 Use small pieces of 'cloud' to fit between the rows of petals, causing them to stand upright.

Water - lily

17 Use Cutter No. B23 for water lily leaf. After cutting out leaf, turn cutter upside down and cut paste again to make a circle.

B23

18 Use Tool No. 2B or Tool No. 4A to lightly frill edges.

19 Mark in veins on front of petal, using Tool 4B.

20 Use a knife and cut out a V after you have completed the edges. This will enable you to cut out a weak patch if one should develop whilst frilling.

21 Finished flower.

No 67

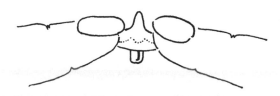

1 Form the calyx by using a pale green paste. Make a tiny ball. Flatten the base of the ball, creating a baby "Mexican hat".

2 Using Cutter No. 67, pick up tiny "Mexican hat" and place over top of cutter. Gently work fingers around cutting edge of cutter. Remove surplus paste and carefully lift out shape.

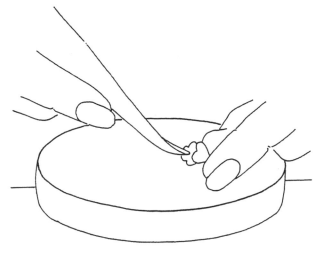

3 With Tool No. 4A, gently stretch petals of calyx on petal pad.

4 Using Tool No. 2B, form a slight hollow in the calyx.

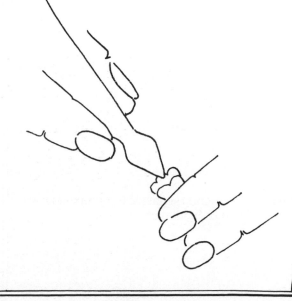

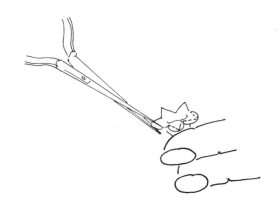

5 Trim the edges of the petals to a point, using a small pair of sharp scissors.

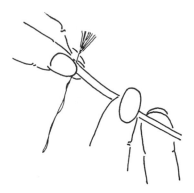

6 Use cotton for stamens. This is illustrated in full under Briar Rose. However, do not use as much cotton as this flower is so tiny. Use ¼ width florist tape to cover the wire.

WHITE VEGETABLE FAT

7 Lightly tip the top of the cotton stamens in white vegetable fat.

8 Carefully dip the tips into red petal dust.

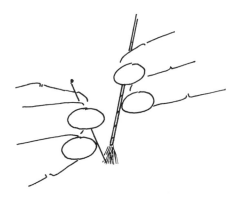

9 Using a hat pin, gently separate the stamens. The stamens should be light in appearance.

10 Using cutter No. B75, cut out five petals in a pale pink or white paste. (N.B. Cover the petals with a light sheet of plastic to prevent them from drying out).

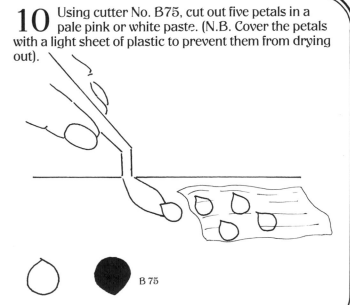

B 75

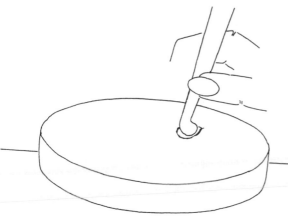

11 Work one petal at a time, using Tool No. 3B. The petals must be very, very thin (transparent). You may wish to shade petals a slightly deeper shade of pink with some petal dust.

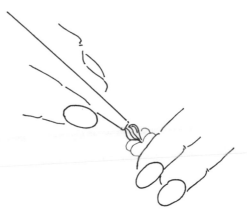

12 Use a paint brush to apply gum glue to calyx.

13 Gently place the first petal in position. The pointed side of the petal goes into the throat of the calyx.
Add the second petal, allowing it to slightly overlap.

14 Add each additional petal, allowing it to slightly overlap the previous petal, until all five petals are in position

15 Using a fine paint brush, carefully place a little gum glue into the centre of flower.

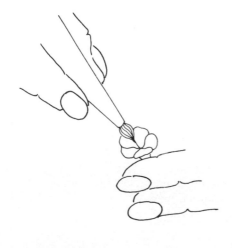

16 Carefully ease the stamens through the centre of the flower.

17 The stamens in position. Rest the blossoms in flower support 3A.

18 The Bud. Make a tiny ball in pink or white paste, and then make a calyx as shown in Step 2. Before attaching calyx, gently mark in petals with sharp craft knife. Secure calyx with egg white.

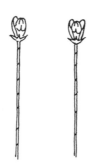

19 To form half opened buds, form centre as above, and add either one or two finely worked single petals to the centre. Add calyx.

L10.

20 Use fine fuse wire, taped in brown florist tape, to create outline for sprig. Add blossoms, buds and leaves as desired, securing with brown tape. Cover remaining stem with brown flower paste to create a realistic effect.

Azalea

1 The Azalea has ten white stamens and a pistil – making a total of eleven. Using very fine fuse wire, secure stamens to taped wire.

2 Using florist tape, cover wire completely.

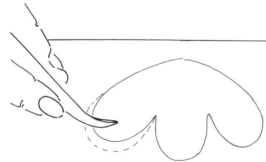

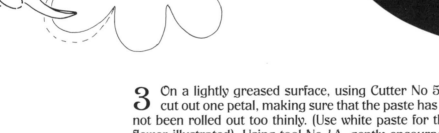

No. 51

3 On a lightly greased surface, using Cutter No 51, cut out one petal, making sure that the paste has not been rolled out too thinly. (Use white paste for the flower illustrated). Using tool No 4A, gently encourage petals to stretch outwards and towards each other, whilst gently fluting the edges with the tool.

4 The worked petal should now look like this.

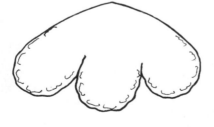

5 Using pink chalk, shade the inside of each petal, making sure to leave the outside edges white.

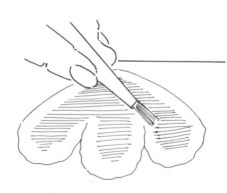

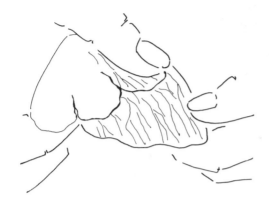

6 Using plastic tulip leaf or other veining aid, press each petal with the coloured side towards the mould to form veins.

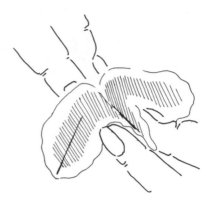

7 Lightly crease the middle petal – see sketch.

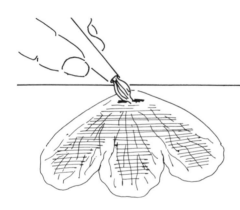

8 Place egg white or gum glue at the base of the petals with a paint brush.

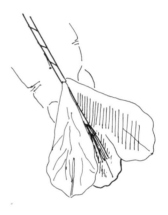

9 Attach stamens to petal at base of petal.

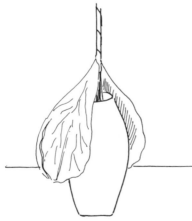

10 Place stamens into macramé bead and allow to rest while you make final petals.

11 Cut out two petals using Cutter No 52. Roll out paste thickly.

No. 52

12 Using tool No 4A, encourage petals to stretch to almost double their size. Lightly frill edges.

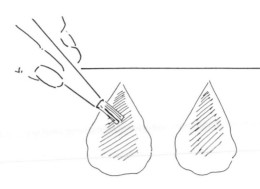

13 Shade petals in pink, remembering to leave outside edges white. N.B. Remember to press against veiner for veins. (Not illustrated).

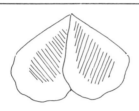

14 Using egg white to secure, overlap petals.

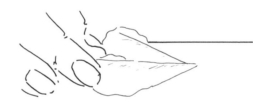

15 Lightly pinch top back of petals to form cup shape.

16 Using egg white or gum glue, place on petals.

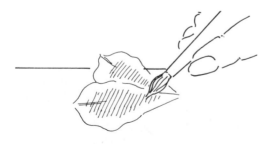

17 Lift up petals from bead and place final two petals in position.

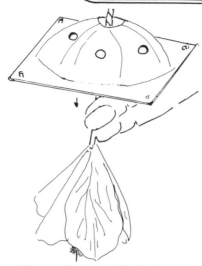

18 Using Flower Support 1A, bring support slowly down towards flower over stem.

19 Turn in upright position and prop up with 'cloud'. N.B. the middle petal of the first three petals is lifted above the petals on either side of it. Using a maroon Koki or a paint brush, mark in dots down the centre petal and on half of both petals on either side of it. N.B. the other petals do not have these markings on them.

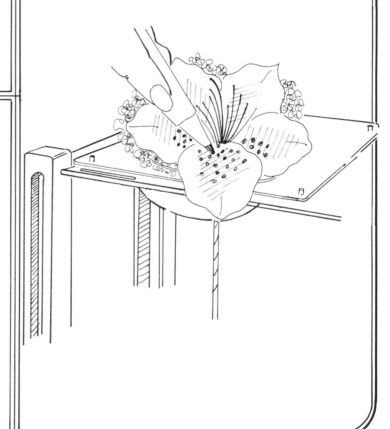

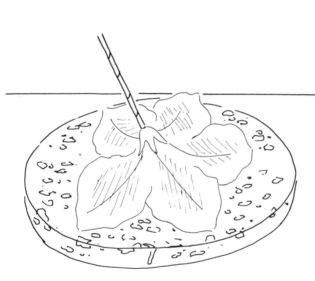

No. 74

20 When flower is completely dry, place on soft sponge and shade the back of the petals pink, remembering not to colour the outside edges. Cut out calyx using cutter No 74. Using egg white or gum glue to secure, gently push calyx through centre down the wire, and place in position.

21 Finished Azalea.

Blushing Bride Protea

1 Use three shades of sewing cotton, a pale pink, a deep maroon and a yellow. Using all three shades together, twist around fingers forming an '8' (see sketch). Twist eight times. Place wire around centre of cotton and twist base firmly to secure. Cut off and firmly grip with very fine fuse wire.

Begin again, just using the pale pink and maroon cotton. Twist eight times and cut off. Firmly grip with fine wire.

Using only pink cotton, carry on with the pink, until you have sufficient stamens for the centre of this flower. Cut off and grip firmly with thin wire.

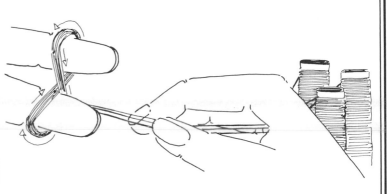

2 Join all the cotton by firmly twisting all the loose wires together. Now use a piece of covered wire, gauge 26. Join the cotton to the stem by covering it with cut florist tape.

3 Using small sharp scissors, cut the centre of each cotton loop.

4 Arrange the cotton stamens evenly. Trim if necessary.

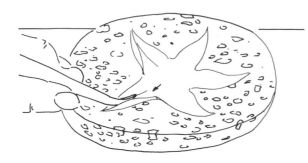

No. 72

5 Using Cutter No. 72, cut out 4 petals. Place on soft sponge, and, using Tool No. 4A, gently pull tool from centre outwards causing petals to crease inwards – see sketch.

6 Using a little egg white or gum glue to secure, place in the centre of the petal. Gently ease petal over stem with curved petals facing inwards towards stamens.

7 Continue as above and add second layer, making sure to position these petals between the other petals. N.B. Before adding third petal, add a tiny piece of green paste to stem to keep the third petal away from the second petal. Work paste on stem at base of previous petal. Continue to add petals with green paste between each additional layer now.

Using Cutter No. 73, cut two petals. Work as above and add to flower, remembering the paste between each petal on the stem.

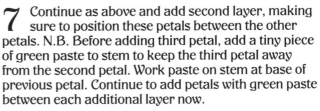

Green paste between petals

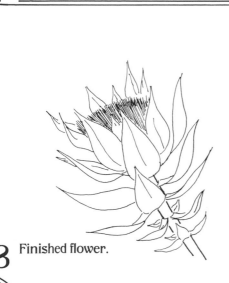

8 Finished flower.

No. 73

Cymbidium

Note: This flower may be made with or without the use of florist wire. Simply omit the wire from all instructions, except the wire on the column in the lip, and proceed as directed.

Only when all petals are completely dry, can this flower be taped together.

ILLUSTRATION 9A: A mould made from instant ceramics using the lip of a real cymbidium.

Carefully remove the lip from the flower. Place the inside of the lip on to the instant ceramics. Shape the base of the mould in order to ensure that it will stand freely. Allow to dry, and then remove lip from the mould.

ILLUSTRATION 9B: Alternatively, the lip of this flower may be supported on a piece of wood which has been shaped to hold the petal. Place tin foil on the support to enable the sides of the lip to dry in an upward position.

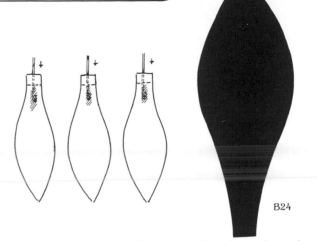

B24

1 Using Cutter No. B24, cut out three lateral sepals. Roll out paste thinly at the top of sepal, leaving a thick base for the insertion of fine, taped, hooked fuse wire. Insert wire now.

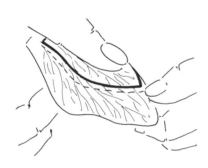

2 Vein each sepal against a veiner or a plastic tulip leaf. Shade both sides of petals with non-toxic chalk.

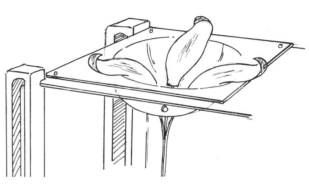

3 Using Flower Former 1A or 1B, place first three lateral sepals in position. Bend wire backwards through the centre of the flower support. One sepal rests in the middle of the back of the support and the other two sepals on either side of it, coming towards the front of the petal former. The sepals should not touch each other. (If you are *not* using wire, take a small piece of paste and make a flat base. Use egg white to secure sepals to base and to each other).

4 Now cut out the two side petals, using Cutter No. B19. Roll out paste thinly at top of petal and leave a thick base for the insertion of fine, taped, hooked wire. Insert wire now.

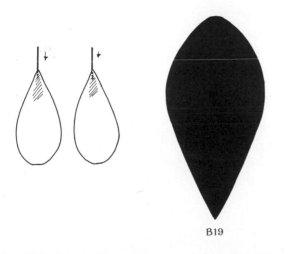

B19

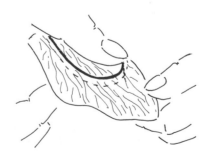

5 Vein petals against veiner. Shade both sides of petals with non-toxic chalk.

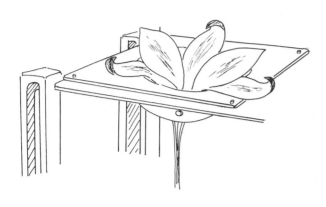

6 Allow the two side petals to rest between the first three sepals.

7 Cut out the lip in the colour of your choice. Cutter No. B3.

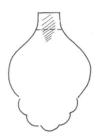

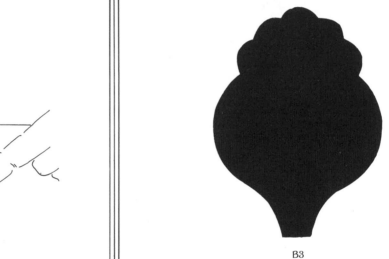

B3

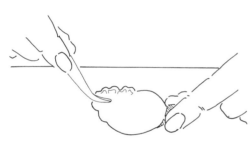

8 Using Tool No. 4A or Tool 2B, gently 'flute' the front part of the lip.

9 Support the lip on the mould, or whatever you have chosen to use. If you use a wooden block, the lip will be facing the other way.

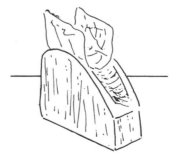

9A

9B

10 Roll a small piece of paste into a 'sausage' shape.

11 Using a sharp knife, slit the 'sausage' in half, ensuring that the top is still joined.

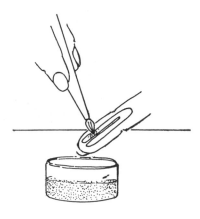

12 Lightly paint with egg white, and then dust on yellow pollen (mixture of coloured maize meal, or colourless gelatin).

Using egg white to secure, carefully place in position in the lip of the orchid.

13 Paint the lip as illustrated, using non-toxic water colours, unless you have an actual orchid to copy.

14 Using a fairly firm wire, (gauge 26) taped, bend the top over slightly as indicated. Check that it is going to fit neatly into the lip of the flower.

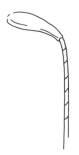

15 With some white paste, cover the bent wire and shape into column. The column should 'seal' the back of the lip.

16 Use Tool 3B to hollow out column.

17 Paint coloured dots on inside of column.

18 Gently ease stem supporting column into the back of the lip. If necessary support with a little 'cloud' until dry.

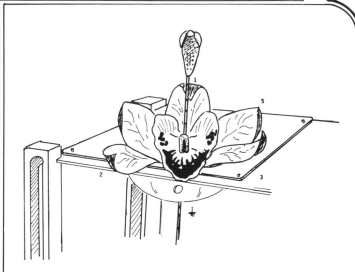

19 If you have not used wire, place lip into sepals, using gum glue to secure.

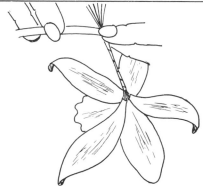

20 If you have wired the sepals and petals and they are completely dry, tape this flower together.

Begin with the three lateral sepals, place in position and tape. Now add the two side petals to the front of the flower and tape securely in position.

Finally add the lip, ensuring that it is in the correct position. Tape securely.

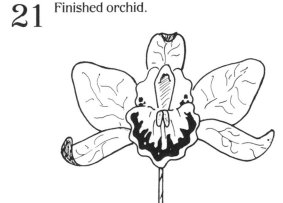

21 Finished orchid.

1 Use a wooden support with a piece of tin foil placed in position to support sides of lip.

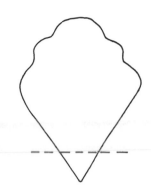

No 25

2 Using cutter No. 25, cut out lip. Trim, if necessary.

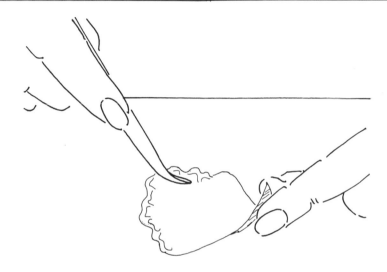

3 Using Tool No. 4A or 2B, gently flute edges of lip.

4 Roll a small piece of paste into a sausage shape.

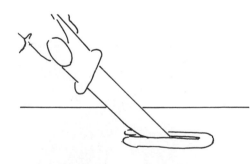

5 Using a sharp knife, slit down the centre.

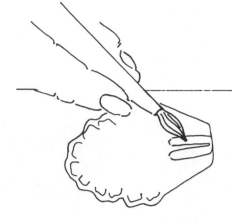

6 Place in the middle of lip, and, using egg white, lightly touch ridges and then add yellow pollen (coloured maize meal or gelatin).

7 Paint and allow to dry completely on petal support.

8 Make column to fit lip – (see instructions in Cymbidium).

9 Join column to lip. Sides of lip should almost cover column.

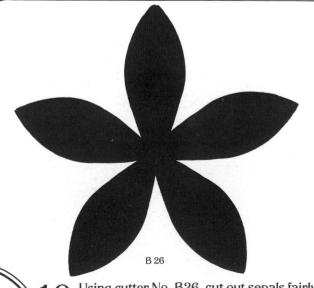

B 26

10 Using cutter No. B26, cut out sepals fairly thickly.

11 Press a veiner, or a dried maize leaf which has had masking tape stuck on the back of it to prevent it from cracking, gently on each of the five sepals.

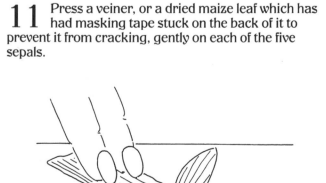

12 Place in petal support 1A, which has been lightly greased with vegetable fat.

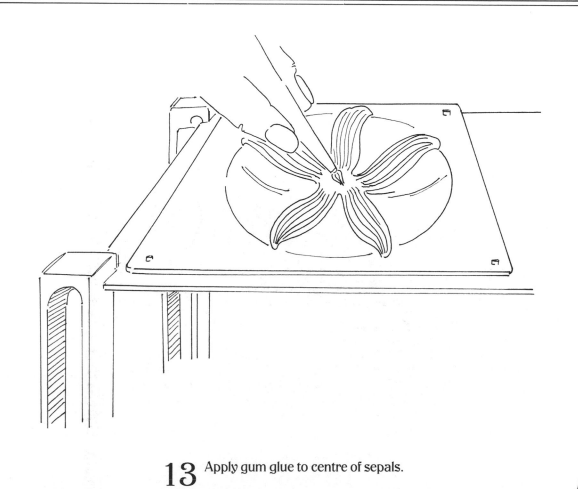

13 Apply gum glue to centre of sepals.

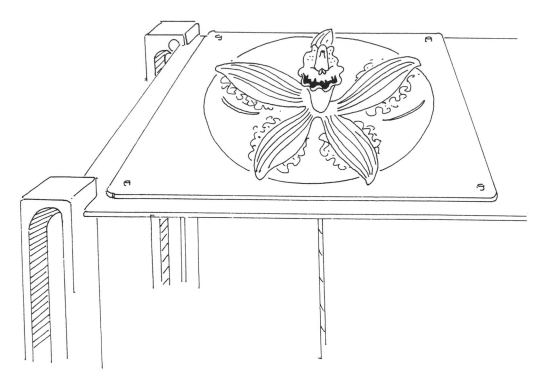

14 Place dried lip into centre of sepals. Support sepals with a little 'cloud'.

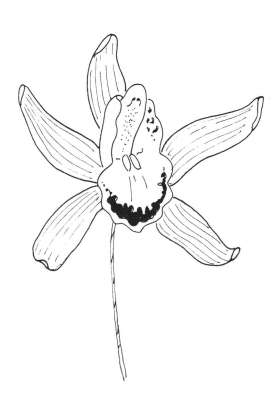

15 Finished orchid.

Day Lily

Note: Day Lilies come in varying shades of yellow to bronze.

Note: These instructions will make a Day Lily approximately half life size.

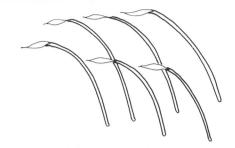

1 Use a piece of fine fuse wire taped and covered with paste to form the pistil. The wire should be slightly longer than the stamens you will use.

2 Use very fine wire (gauge 30) covered in white florist tape, for stamens. Use food colouring to shade stamens to desired colour. Bend into shape. Make anthers out of a little gum paste, dip into pollen.

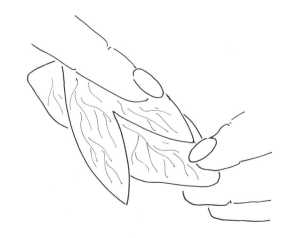

3 Using half width florist tape, join stamens to pistil.

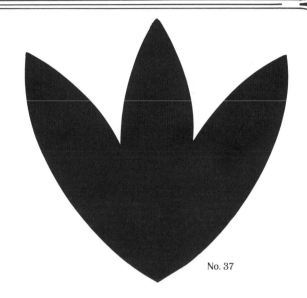

No. 37

4 Cut out one petal using Cutter No. 37.

5 Press against veiner.

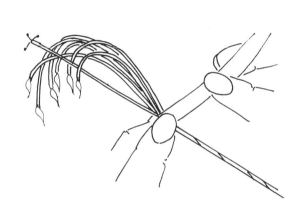

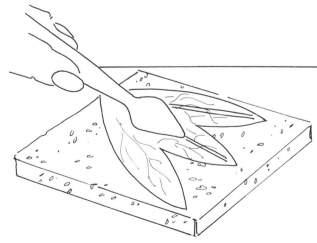

6 Place petal on petal pad, and using Tool No. 5B (double split side), pull tool over petals from outside to centre of petals.

Day Lily

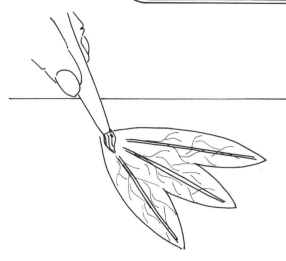

7 Tip base of petal with gum glue.

8 Allow petals to hang down and gently ease around stamens, allowing the petal to join at base.

9 Use a little gum glue to join petals.

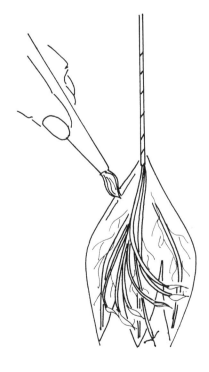

10 Join petals at base.

11 Press each petal over veiner.

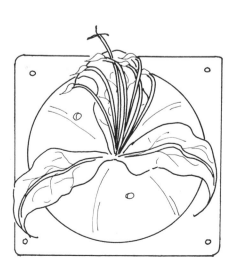

No. 21

12 Cut three more petals, using cutter No. 21.

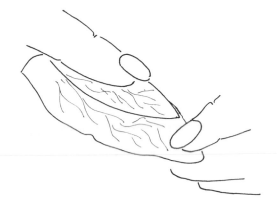

13 Press each petal over veiner

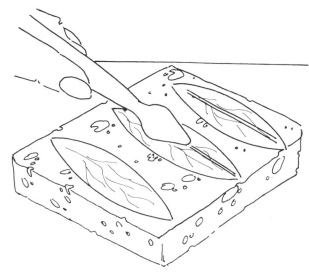

14 Place petals on foam, and, using tool No. 5B, work from top to base of each petal to form ridge in petal.

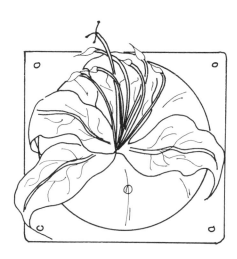

15 Now add additional petals between the initial row, using gum glue to secure.

16 Use 'cloud' to support petals.

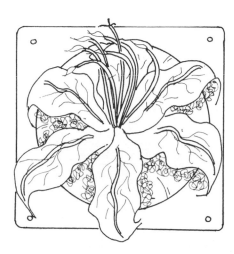

17 To make the bud, roll a small amount of paste the size of a marble into a ball.

$\mathcal{D}$ay $\mathcal{L}$ily

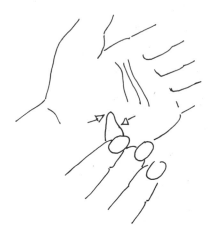

18 Roll in the palm of your hand to form pointed tip with a wider base.

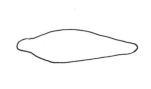

19 Shape of bud.

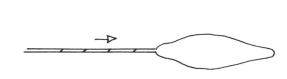

20 Use fairly firm taped wire, tipped with gum glue, and gently ease into blunt end of bud.

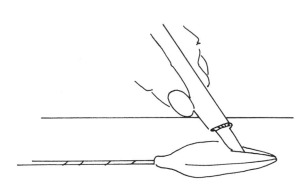

21 Use a sharp knife and carefully cut grooves into bud to create a petal effect. Shade as desired.

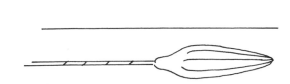

22 The bud.

23 Finished flower.

Freesia

1 Using fine fuse wire, join four fine stamens together. One stamen must be slightly longer than the other three forming the pistil. Cover stem with florist tape ¼ gauge.

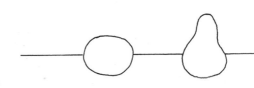

2 Roll a small ball of paste between the size of a marble and a pea into a pear shape.

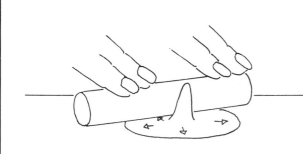

3 Flatten outside edges with fingers and then a roller.

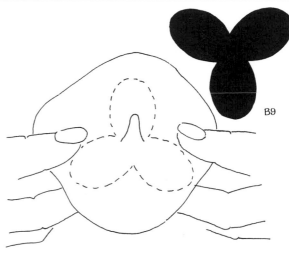

B9

4 Holding Cutter B9, in your hand, ensure pointed part of hat is over the middle of cutter, press fingers over edge of cutter causing petals to be cut out forming a trumpet-like shape of even thickness all round.

5 Place trumpet into Mexican Petal Pad, and using Tool 10A continue to work petals until they are even, thin and 'cupped'.

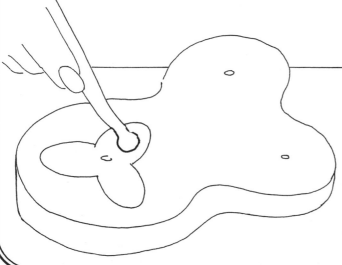

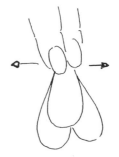

6 Tool 10A and then 10B will help deepen the throat. Allow petals to hang down and roll base of petals backwards and forwards between fingers, thinning the trumpet.

Freesia

7 Gently ease stamens through petals and allow to hang down over Handy Holder.

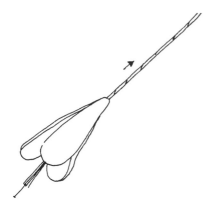

8 Cut out three petals using cutter No. B70. Cover with soft plastic to prevent drying.

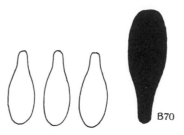

B70

9 Place petals on soft foam, and, using tool No. 3B, gently hollow out each petal.

10 Place outside petals between first layer of petals allowing petals to hang downwards. Allow petals to dry.

11 Use cutter No. 23 and green paste. Cut out the calyx and place it on the flower as illustrated.

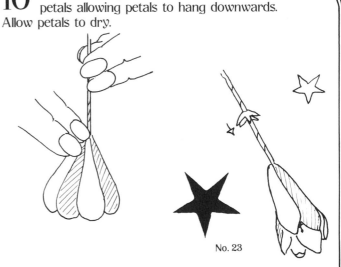

No. 23

Note: Make a number of flowers, bearing in mind that tiny buds appear at the end of the stem and larger flowers are on the lower part of the stem.

To make buds, simply roll a small ball of paste into a tear drop shape. Use a sharp craft knife to mark in lines to indicate petals. Add a small piece of hooked, taped fuse wire and a calyx. Allow to dry.

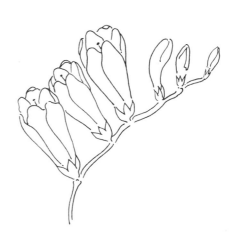

12 When all flowers and buds are dry, begin assembling spray with small buds, first carefully taping the buds together. Gradually add the larger flowers to the spray.

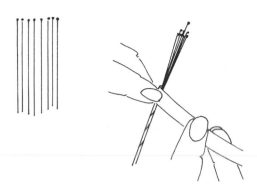

1 Using very fine taped fuse wire as the pistil, tape nine stamens to it. The pistil should be slightly longer than the stamens. The heads of the stamens should be cut off.

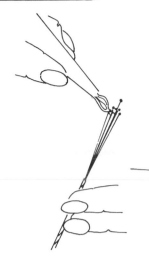

2 Lightly tip the tops of the stamens with gum glue using a paint brush.

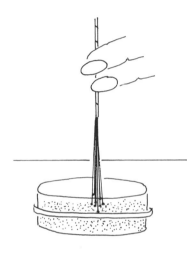

3 Dip into a mixture of white pollen. (This can be made from maize meal).

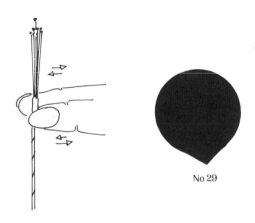

No 29

4 Using Cutter No 29, cut out one petal and twist back and forth, covering the join of the stamens to the wire.

5 Now cut out several other petals with Cutter No 29, covering them with light plastic or a plastic lid to prevent drying.

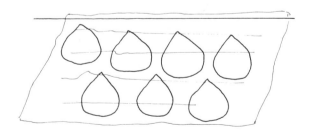

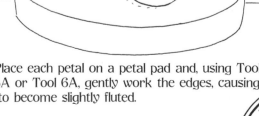

6 Place each petal on a petal pad and, using Tool 3A or Tool 6A, gently work the edges, causing them to become slightly fluted.

Double Fuchsia

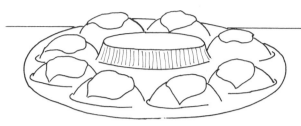

7 Place worked petals over upside-down artist's tray to partially dry.

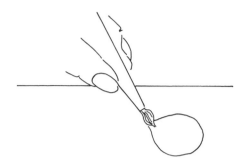

8 Place a tiny bit of egg white or gum glue on the base of four petals and join them to the stem, one at a time.

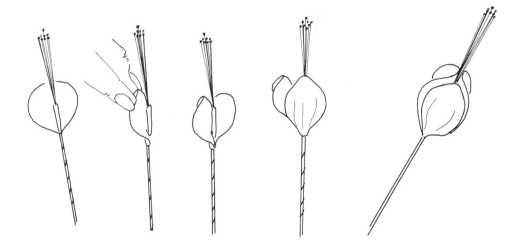

9 Bend back each petal as you attach it to the stem.

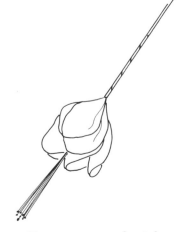

10 Place two rows of petals on the stem in this way.

11 Now fold the base of the remaining petals together – causing a cone-like effect.

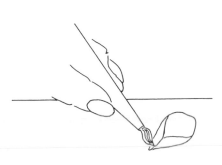

12 Using a little egg white or gum glue to secure, attach these petals to the previous layers of petals until you have a sufficiently full flower.

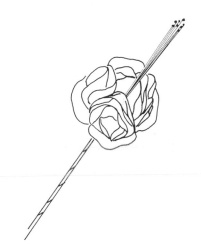

13 Final row of petals.

14 Using a contrasting shade of flower paste, roll into a ball about the size of a pea or a small marble. Flatten outside edges of the ball, leaving a peaked centre forming a Mexican hat.

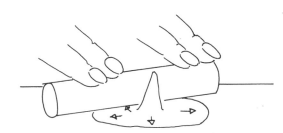

15 Using a roller, roll the outside edges of the Mexican hat until evenly and thinly distributed. Make sure the Mexican hat is big enough to fit over the cutter.

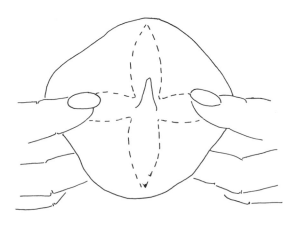

No 11

16 Holding Cutter No 11 in your hand, place Mexican hat over the cutter, ensuring the pointed part of hat is over the middle of cutter. Gently press fingers over edge of cutter. Remove surplus paste.

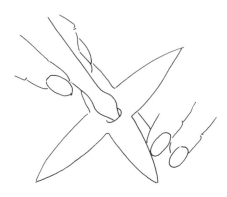

17 Using Tool 2B, gently open throat of calyx.

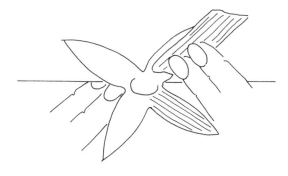

18 Vein each sepal using dried maize leaf or other veiner.

19 Place a little gum glue into the centre of the calyx. Gently ease petals into the calyx by pushing the wire through the centre of the calyx.

20 Bend sepals backwards, away from petals. To complete the calyx, use a little green paste to form a small teardrop shape. Ease down the stem to join back of the flower.

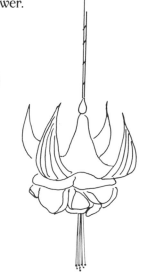

21 Finished fuchsia.

Holly Spray

Note: Holly may be made using a plain, very dark green paste.

The illustration given below is of a variegated holly. The outside of the leaf is a soft yellow and the middle a darkish green.

No 57   No 58

1 Cut out 2 holly leaves, a big one in the pale shade and a smaller one in green. Use Cutter No's 57 and 58.

2 Place the small leaf on the bigger leaf.

3 Place the leaves on a petal pad. Using tool 3B, work the edges, encouraging the leaf to form cupped sides.

4 Use Tool 4B and mark in the veins.

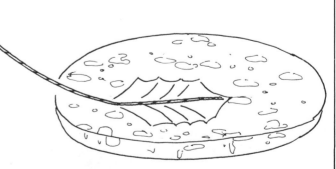

5 Turn the leaf upside down. Bend a piece of taped wire to angle required. Apply gum glue to wire and place over back of leaf from tip to base. Alternatively, insert wire into paste by leaving a slightly thicker base in the leaf.

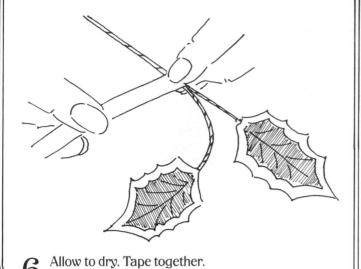

6 Allow to dry. Tape together.

7 Roll out tiny red berries, attach to fine taped hooked wire in small bunches of 1's, 2's, 3's and 5's.

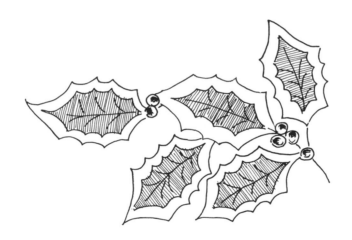

8 Add red berries to stem at intervals. Use florist tape to secure.

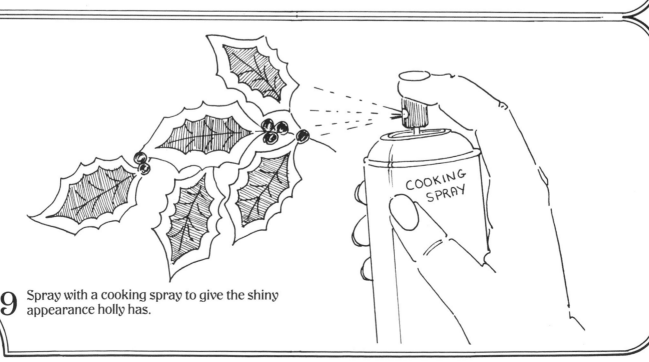

COOKING SPRAY

9 Spray with a cooking spray to give the shiny appearance holly has.

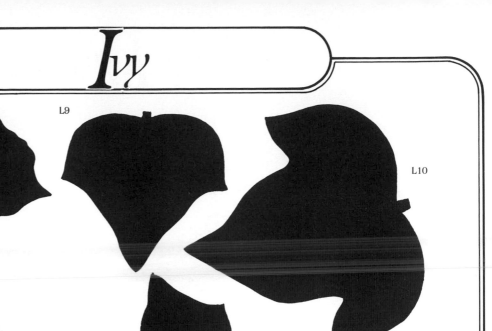

L8   L9   L10

No. 32

L12

1 Use white paste for these leaves.
Use any of Cutters L8, L9, L10, L12 and No. 32. It is interesting to note that on the larger variety of ivy, small and larger leaves are on the same stem.

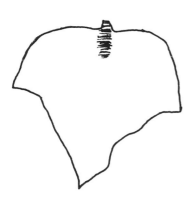

2 Roll out paste carefully, leaving it slightly thicker at the base of the leaf. Only one leaf may be cut out at a time.

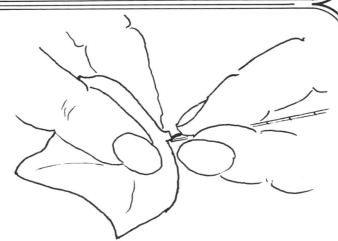

3 Using a fine, taped, wire with a bent hook in it, hold the leaf between your thumb and index finger and carefully ease the wire into the paste. Make sure that the wire does not penetrate the outsides of the paste. Apply a little egg white to base of wire to secure. Do not allow egg white to touch surface of paste.

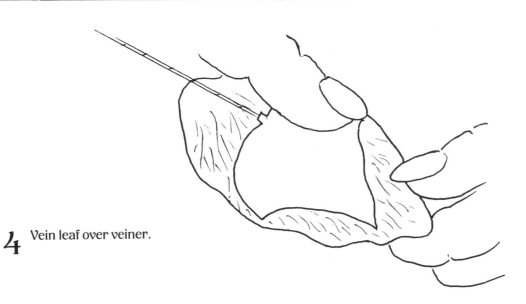

4 Vein leaf over veiner.

Ivy

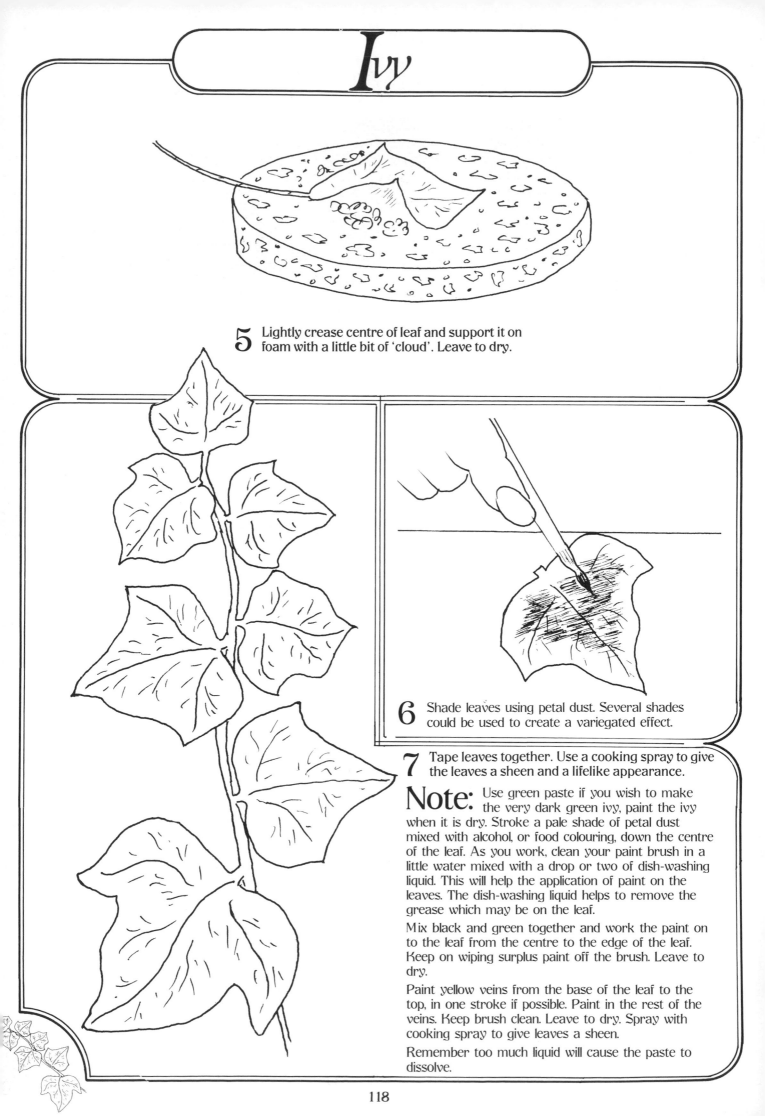

5 Lightly crease centre of leaf and support it on foam with a little bit of 'cloud'. Leave to dry.

6 Shade leaves using petal dust. Several shades could be used to create a variegated effect.

7 Tape leaves together. Use a cooking spray to give the leaves a sheen and a lifelike appearance.

Note: Use green paste if you wish to make the very dark green ivy, paint the ivy when it is dry. Stroke a pale shade of petal dust mixed with alcohol, or food colouring, down the centre of the leaf. As you work, clean your paint brush in a little water mixed with a drop or two of dish-washing liquid. This will help the application of paint on the leaves. The dish-washing liquid helps to remove the grease which may be on the leaf.

Mix black and green together and work the paint on to the leaf from the centre to the edge of the leaf. Keep on wiping surplus paint off the brush. Leave to dry.

Paint yellow veins from the base of the leaf to the top, in one stroke if possible. Paint in the rest of the veins. Keep brush clean. Leave to dry. Spray with cooking spray to give leaves a sheen.

Remember too much liquid will cause the paste to dissolve.

Magnolia

B43

1 Use white or cream paste for this flower depending on the variety you wish to make. The shape of the petals, may vary.

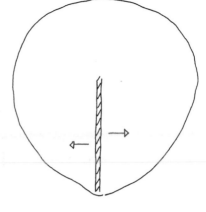

2 If you wish to wire each petal, roll out the paste leaving a thin ridge of paste for the wire in the centre of the petal. A roller with a small diameter will be helpful for this.

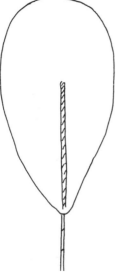

3 Insert taped wire, gauge 26 as far as it will go into the ridge of the petal.

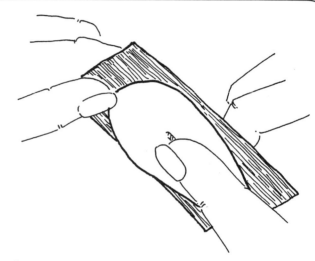

4 Vein over corn leaf veiner.

5 Carefully shape top of petals, either lightly frilling the edges, or pinching their edges between your fingers.

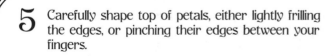

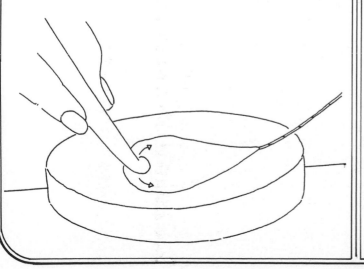

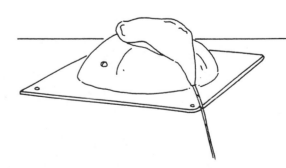

6 Place petal over petal former 1A and leave to dry completely.

7 Depending on the flower you wish to make, you would use mauve, green, or cream paste for your centre. Form a cone shape and insert a gauge 26 taped, hooked wire, into the cone.

8 Now use tweezers to form the inside ridges on the cone. The ridges should be as close together as possible. Work from the base to the tip of the cone, making what appears to be a lot of tightly closed stamens.

9 Turn the centre upside-down. Apply gum glue to base of cone. Have numerous middle sections of lightly shaded mauve stamens ready cut. Place these over the base of the cone as close together as possible. Leave to dry upside-down.

10 Using petal dust mixed with a little alcohol, paint the top of the centre white, if centre is mauve or, light brown, if centre is green or cream.

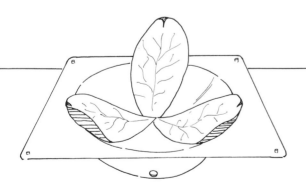

11 If wire is not to be used in petals, assemble flower in support 1A, evenly spacing three petals, ensuring they overlap at the base.

12 Now add the next layer of petals.

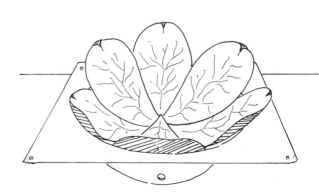

13 Add the final layer of petals.

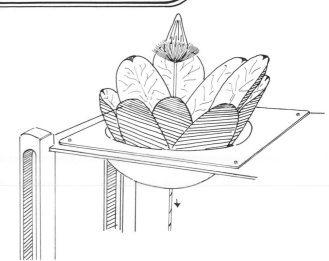

14 Apply gum glue to the centre of the flower and gently ease your centre into position.

15 Support petals with a little 'cloud' as desired.

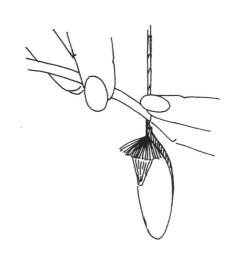

16 If you have wired each petal, use florist tape cut in ¼ width, to tape petal to stamens. First three petals and then the next three petals and, finally the last row of petals.

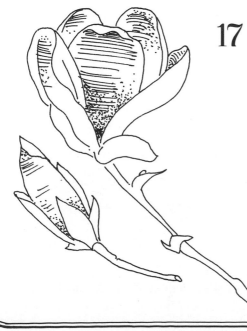

17 A finished flower and bud. Another magnolia specimen.

Note: When the flower is dry, you may wish to shade the outside petals with non-toxic chalk. Be careful not to allow the coloured chalk on to the white side of the petals.

It is interesting to note that there are numerous species of this flower. Some having different shaped petals. The shading and centres also vary.

Maidenhair Fern

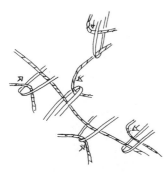

1 Using very fine covered fuse wire, painted brown, and brown florist tape shredded into quarters, firmly tape central skeleton stem into desired shape. Cut lengths of wire about 2 or 3 cm long, and, using more fine florist tape begin to form skeleton for maidenhair fern. Shape should taper at the end and widen at the base.

2 The skeleton.

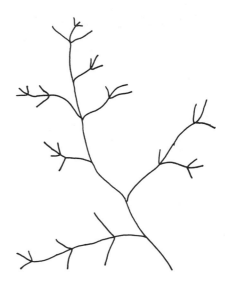

Note: The skeleton from dried maidenhair fern may also be used, but this will have to remain flat on the cake when displayed.

L16

3 Using Cutter No L16, cut out as many leaves as needed. Cover petals with soft plastic or a plastic lid to prevent drying out.

4 Using Tool 4A, work the leaves, creating a veined effect on them. Dried maize leaf is an excellent veiner.

Note: An artist's palette-knife can be used to flatten the leaves to make a variety of shapes, which make the fern more interesting.

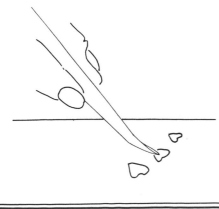

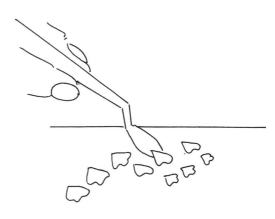

5 Use an artist's palette-knife to pick up the leaves.

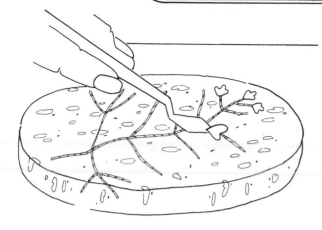

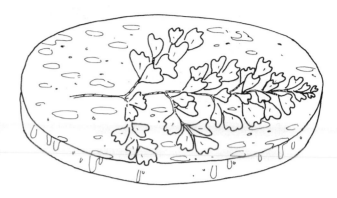

6 Place skeleton on a piece of foam. Apply egg white or gum glue to stem where you wish to place the leaves.
It is a good idea to hide any untidy joins with a leaf.

7 The built up stem.
When the leaves are completely dry, lightly spray them with a cooking spray. This gives the leaves a life-like lustre.

8 Maidenhair fern.

Oak Leaves & Acorns

L14

L13

L15

1 Use cutters Nos L13, L14 and L15 for the leaves. A spray of oak leaves would be in varied sizes.

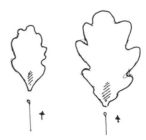

2 Roll out paste thinly for top of leaf, allowing base of leaf to be fairly thick in the centre. Cut out the leaves. Insert fine taped fuse wire, which has a closed hook in it, into the "thick base".

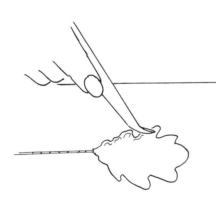

3 Using Tool 4A, work the edges to create a slightly fluted effect.

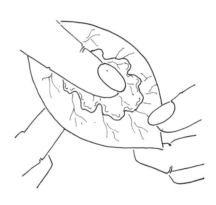

4 Vein leaves with a leaf veiner, or mark in veins with Tool 4B.

5 Allow all leaves to dry completely. Use petal dust to shade leaves. Pass the leaves through some steam if you do not want them to have the sheen that a cooking spray creates.

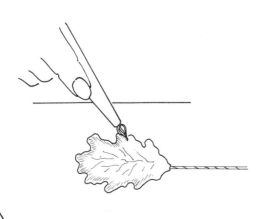

6 To make acorn, use light brown paste or green paste, depending on preference and the colour of the leaves.
Roll a ball of paste slightly smaller than a marble, and, using Tool No 5A, open the throat of the ball to form the cup to hold the acorn.

7 Use Tool No 6A to round off inside of shell.

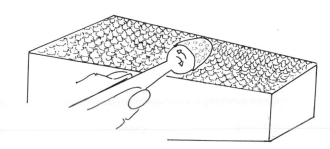

8 Leave Tool 6A in the centre of the 'cup'. Use the finest grater you have and gently roll the 'cup' backwards and forwards on the grater, causing the desired effect.

9 Now take another ball of paste and roll it into an egg shape, ensuring that the base will fit into the 'cup'. Add taped wire to base.

10 Apply egg white to 'cup'.

11 Place acorn in position.

12 Finished spray, taped together.

*O*range *B*lossom

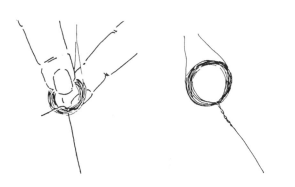

1 Using fine fuse wire taped in white florist tape, cover tip with a little white paste, which will form the pistil of the flower.

2 Now using white cotton for stamens, wind it over your fingers (as for briar rose). Secure base with fine fuse wire.

3 Cut circle and join cotton stamens to pistil. Cover with ¼ tape to neaten.

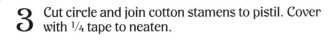

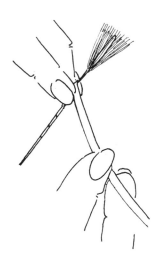

4 Use small sharp scissors to trim stamens.

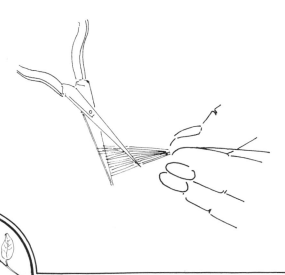

5 Dip cotton stamens into melted white vegetable fat.

WHITE VEGETABLE FAT

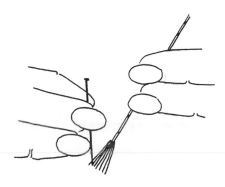

6 When set, carefully separate stamen tops with a pin. Remember, these stamens appear to touch each other and stand upright. Shade pistil yellow/green and the stamens light brown.

B17

7 Using cutter No. B17 roll out paste leaving a bit of thickness in the centre of the petals.

8 Cut out petals.

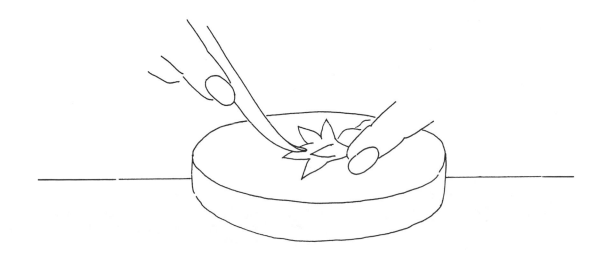

9 Place petals on petal pad and using Tool 4A carefully thin petals.

Orange Blossom

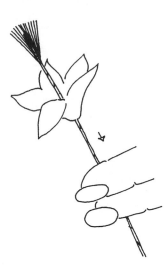

10 Apply a little gum glue to stamen base, and gently ease into position.

11 Using Cutter No. 23 and then No. 67 add calyx to blossom.

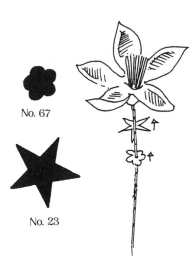

No. 67

No. 23

Note: It is interesting to note that in a single orange tree the blossoms found in it can have, four, five or six petals. However, orange blossoms with five petals are the most predominant.

12 Make a few buds which should be shaded a pinky/brown. Tape into spray with a few bright yellow/green leaves.

Petrea

Note:

Use purple or white paste.

No. 43

1 Roll paste into Mexican hat shape. Use Cutter No. 43.

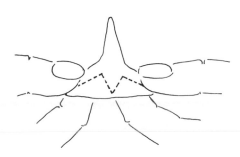

2 Place paste over the centre of the cutter and gently work fingers around the cutter, causing it to cut out the sepals.

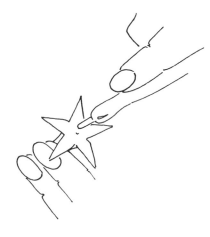

3 Now using Tool 2A, make a tiny throat in the flower. Be careful not to widen it.

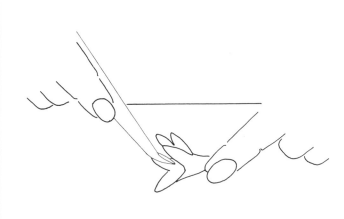

4 Use Tool 4A to work the sepals until they are evenly thin.

5 Now using an artist's palette-knife, flatten the sepals causing the sharp tip to appear slightly rounded.

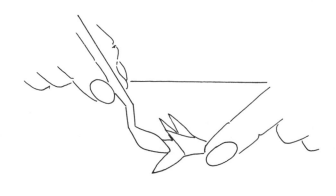

6 Use small sharp scissors and round off the sepals.

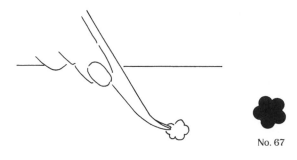

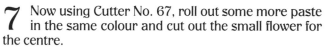

No. 67

7 Now using Cutter No. 67, roll out some more paste in the same colour and cut out the small flower for the centre.

Use Tool No. 4A and gently press into each petal.

8 Place a white stamen in the centre of the flower and secure with a little egg white at the back of the flower.

10 Make several flowers in the same way, and make several more flowers, leaving off the centre flower. Here all that is necessary is a stamen covered with a tiny piece of paste in the same colour to form a tiny bud-like centre.

To make smaller flowers for the top of the spray, use Cutter B60. These tiny flowers will not have the small centre flower in them.

Make as many flowers as required and carefully tape into a spray.

B 60

9 Now ease the little flower into the larger sepals, allowing the flower to sit level on top of the sepals.

P*rotea*

1 Use a very heavy wire (gauge 22), which has been taped, for this flower. Bend it into a round hook.

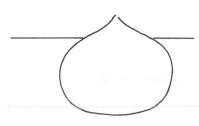

2 Use a fairly large piece of old modelling paste or fondant, about the size of a ping pong ball, and roll into a ball. Gently create a pointed effect in the centre.

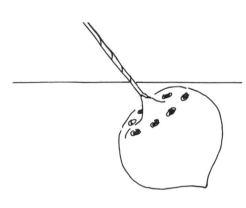

3 Add egg white or gum glue to hook. Ease hook into the paste and ensure that it is held securely by the modelling paste. Make a number of holes in the base of the modelling paste to help drying. If you do not do this, you will find that the large piece of paste/fondant will crack, spoiling your flower. Allow centre to dry completely (24 hours).

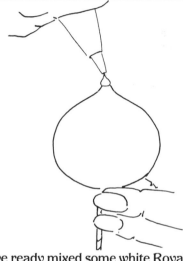

4 Have ready mixed some white Royal Icing (soft peak consistency). This is to be placed into an icing bag with a No. 1 or a No. 0 icing tube in it.

Begin at the top centre of your flower and pipe little peaks all around the top of the centre.

5 Work all the way around the centre trying to keep the points even and fine. No space should be visible between each piped point.

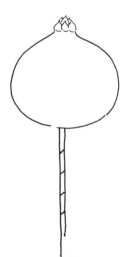

6 When you have covered about a third of the centre with icing, begin to lengthen your icing strokes. You may find it easier to work upside-down by simply holding the centre above you. Leave to dry.

Protea

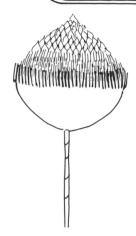

7 Your last two rows may be piped in a very pale green. These strokes should not touch the centre, but should be encouraged to stand away from it.

B 54

8 Using Cutter B54, cut out two or three petals at a time until you have made enough petals to completely surround the centre twice. Do not attempt to cut out all the petals at once. Cover petals with plastic to prevent drying out when you are not working with them.

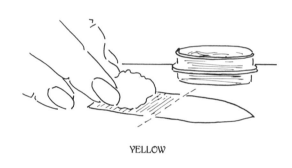

YELLOW

9 With a piece of cotton wool, shade the bottom half of each petal with yellow non-toxic chalk.

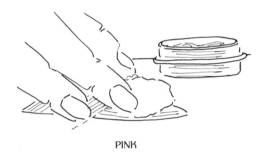

PINK

10 Using a salmon pink non-toxic chalk, shade the top half of each petal. Shade the back of the petals pink.

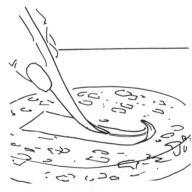

11 Place each petal on a piece of foam and, using tool 4A, gently pull tool over petal, beginning at the top and working to base. Petal will curl slightly. The tool should leave a slight indentation in the petal.

12 Place petals over a piece of corrugated plastic or something similar and allow to partially dry.

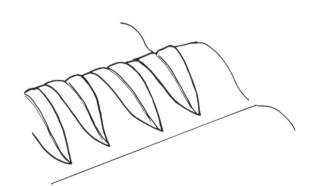

13 Brush egg white or gum glue at the base of the royal icing points.

14 Place the first row of petals around the centre. Keep them even.

15 Position the second row of petals between the first row of petals, and place them just a bit higher than the last row, say 3 mm.

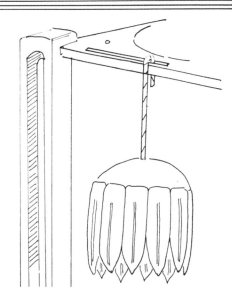

16 Allow petals to hang down as you work.

17 Using Cutter B53, cut out sufficient petals to make a third row. Repeat method.

B 53

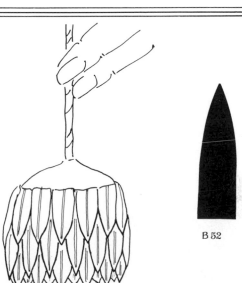

18 Now use Cutter B52 and make another complete row of petals around the base of the flower.

B 52

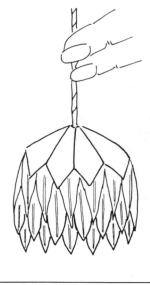

19 Using Cutter cut out sufficient petals to cover back of flower.

No. 80

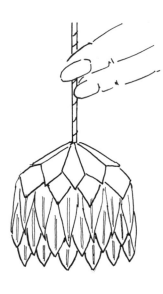

20 Now use Cutter and cut out more petals, which will fit between the previous row.

No. 78

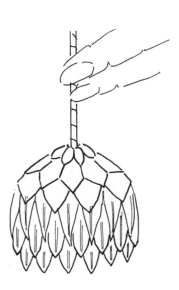

21 Add the final row of petals using Cutter. Ensure that the back of the flower is completely covered.

No. 77

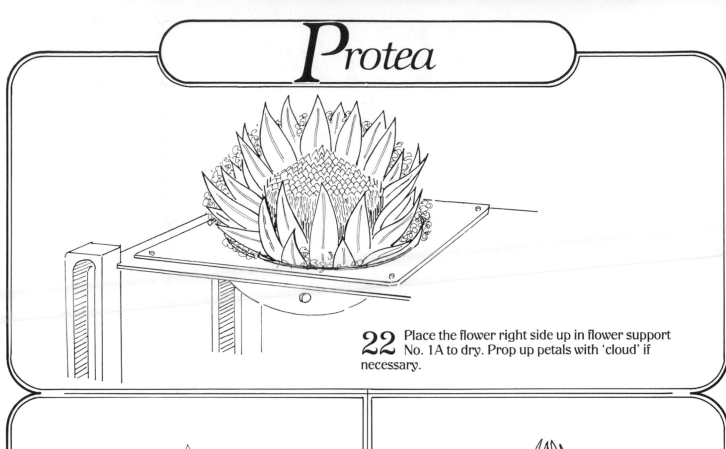

22 Place the flower right side up in flower support No. 1A to dry. Prop up petals with 'cloud' if necessary.

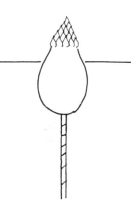

23 To make a bud, shape the plastic icing into a cone shape. Pipe in white 'stamens' as above, working over ⅓ of the cone.

24 Proceed as before. However, allow inside petals, i.e. first row, to meet at the top of the bud, creating a slightly 'closed' effect.

25 Finished flower.

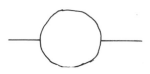

1 Begin by making a ball of paste about the size of a marble or larger. Naturally, the size of bud you wish to make will determine the size of the 'ball' you begin with.

2 Now pick up the ball, and, using your fingers, flatten the top half of the ball. This is important.

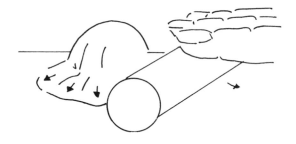

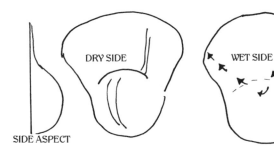

3 Place the paste on to your worktop surface. Using your roller, roll the flattened edges out evenly, working from the thick part of the paste to the outside.

Try to keep the shape of the petal even. Make sure edges are thin, but not broken.

4 Pick up the paste with the wet side facing you, i.e. the side which has been on the board. (See sketch to indicate what this should look like from side view. – Notice the bulge is formed more noticeably on the dry side of the paste).

5 Now with the wet side facing you, begin to roll the flattened edge from the top of the right hand side. Make the rolling as close together as possible.

Roll the paste in the direction of the bulge. Roll the paste over the bulge and now change direction and roll the paste up towards the top left hand corner.

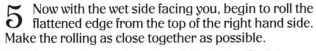

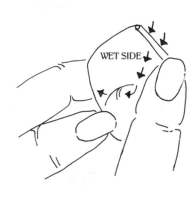

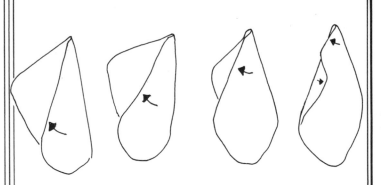

6 If you want to make a very closed bud you will only require this part of the flower. (See progressive stages of rolling the bud).

7 However, for a slightly more open bud, the last bit of paste rolled up is then turned backwards to create the impression of a petal beginning to unfold.

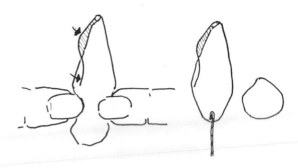

8 Neaten the shape of your bud by simply twisting off the base of the bud. Return excess ball of paste to plastic bag.

To wire bud, place a hooked, taped wire into the base and allow to dry.

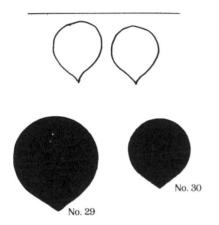

No. 30

No. 29

9 If you wish to add one or two petals to the bud, cut out a petal using a cutter appropriate to the size of the bud you are making. Cutter No. 29 or 30 can be used in this case.

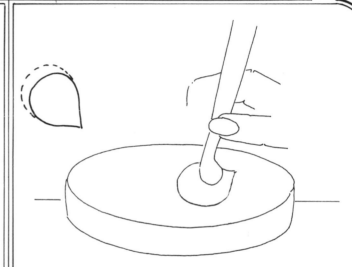

10 Place the petal on a petal pad, and, using Tool 3A or 6A, roll the rounded edge outwards, creating a slightly longer petal which is also thin on the edge.

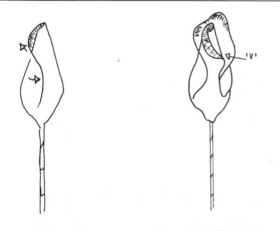

'V'

11 The first petal is placed over the bent back petal on the centre of the bud, forming a 'V' shape. The top of this petal is very slightly bent backwards.

The second petal, if used, would be placed over the 'V'. The tip of this petal would also be bent slightly backwards.

12 Use Cutter No. 72 for the calyx. This can be bent backwards, or, if a closed bud is desired, the calyx should be closed over the bud.

Note: If you intend making a full rose, it is essential that you DO NOT bend back the petals as directed in Step 11.

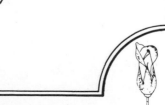

Rose Calyx

Note: You may either make the calyx flat, or use the Mexican hat method.

No. 72

1 Using a dull green paste, roll out calyx. Using Cutter No. 72, or smaller, depending on the size, cut out calyx.

2 If you wish to make a hollowed out calyx, roll your paste into a ball about the size of a marble. Flatten the edges to form a Mexican Hat.

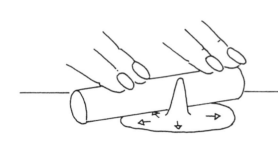

3 Use a small roller to achieve a good result.

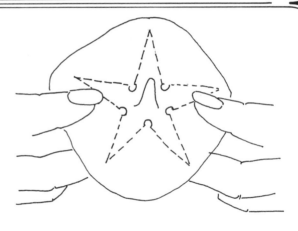

4 Holding Cutter No. 72 in your hand, place Mexican hat over the cutter ensuring that the pointed part of the paste, is over the middle of the cutter. Gently press fingers over edge of cutter. Remove surplus paste.

5 Using a small sharp knife or a craft knife, make two small incisions into the calyx from the centre towards the pointed part of the sepals. Each sepal should have at least two slits in it. Using finger tips, lightly pinch the tips of the sepals.

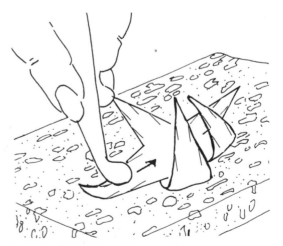

6 Now place the calyx on a petal pad, and using either Tool 3A or 10A, pull the tool over the point of the sepals towards the centre, causing the sepals to curl inwards.

7 If you have cut out a flat calyx, use Tool 6A to 'cup' the centre of the calyx.

8 Apply gum glue to centre of calyx. Attach to bud or rose.

10 Calyx on bud showing hip.

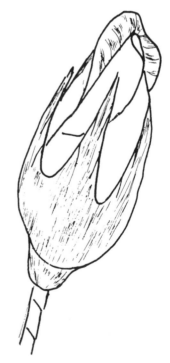

9 Roll a small piece of green paste into a ball and place this under the calyx to form the rose hip. Work the hip into the calyx neatly.

Note: If you wish to fold the sepals back, do not place glue over entire surface. Apply white petal dust to inside of sepals.
If you wish to have the calyx almost cover the bud, apply glue to the full length of the sepals.

Rose Leaves

Note: White petals dust may be applied to the underside of the finished leaves. This will mean that it is not necessary to have two shades of paste.

However, should you wish to use two colours, ensure that the size of the paste used is equal. Remember to allow a little thickness at the base of the leaf for the insertion of wire.

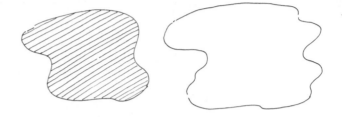

1 Roll out the green paste and the pale paste separately.

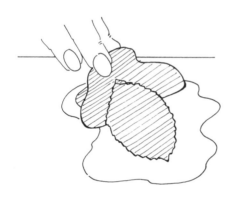

B50

B49

B48

2 Place the dark shade over the light paste. Using Cutter No. B48, cut out the top leaf. Remove surplus paste separately – returning correct colours to main balls of paste.

3 Insert fine, taped, hooked wire into thick base of leaf. Secure with gum glue making sure gum glue does not touch paste, or it will leave a mark on the icing. Continue cutting out four smaller leaves, using first Cutter No. B49 and then B50. (You may prefer to only use B49).

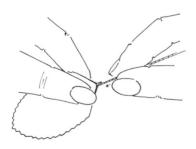

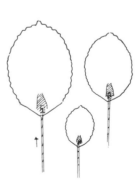

4 Wired leaf.

Rose Leaves

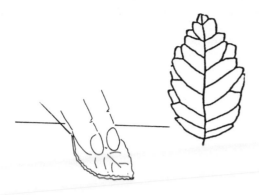

5 Use a rose leaf veiner to vein leaves.

6 Shape leaf by lightly creasing the centre of leaf inwards.

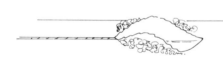

7 Slightly lift up sides of leaf and support with 'cloud'. Leave to dry.

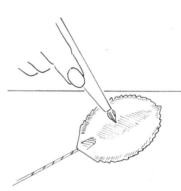

8 When leaves are dry, shade with green petal dust. Use a yellow dust down the centre of the leaves. You may then like to add a darker green to the edges of the leaves. Shade the serrated edges with a red/brown petal dust.
Finally use white petal dust for the underside of the leaves.

9 Tape leaves together. The side leaves should almost join the central stem. The largest leaf is at the top working down to the smaller leaves. Spray with cooking spray ± 35cm away from leaves. Alternatively, hold leaves in the steam from a kettle. It is a good idea to spray leaves in advance. This allows the sheen to fade slightly, giving a more realistic effect.

*S*weet *P*ea

1 Tape Florist wire in green (gauge 24). Cover tip with paste.

2 Using Cutter No. 29, make the centre. The centre of the sweet pea is usually a paler shade than the other petals. Use a little gum glue to attach centre to stem. Allow petal to appear slightly open when it meets in front. This forms the inside 'beak' petal.

Inside 'beak' petal

No 29

3 Using Cutter No 41, cut out one petal. This petal will form the middle petal, which should actually be two separate petals.
In order to create this effect, simply use a cutter with a sharp point, e.g. arum lily cutter No 55, and cut out the centre, forming a V in the middle petal.
Using a fluting Tool 4A or 2B, gently frill the edges of the petal. Make sure you do not leave 'ridge marks' in the petal.

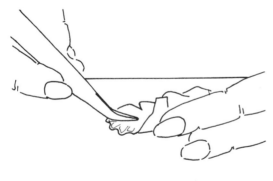

No 55

No 41

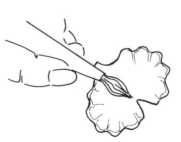

4 Using gum glue to secure, attach to centre of flower. (See Step 5).

Middle 'beak' petals

5 You now have the middle 'beak'. Leave to dry.

The 'hood' petal

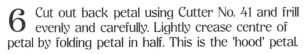

No 41

6 Cut out back petal using Cutter No. 41 and frill evenly and carefully. Lightly crease centre of petal by folding petal in half. This is the 'hood' petal.

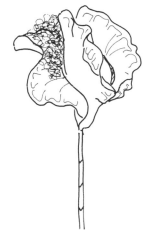

7 Now attach the centre to the back petal by placing a little gum glue at the base of the petal, making sure that the middle petal does not rest on the back petal. This petal must stand away. Use 'cloud' or sponge foam chips to ensure this, if necessary.

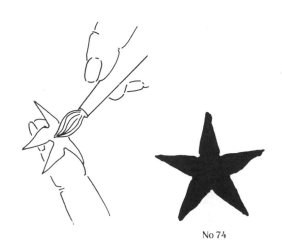

No 74

8 Using Cutter No. 74, attach the calyx to flower with a little gum glue.

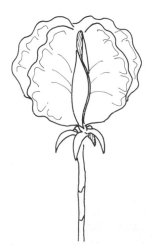

9 Finished sweet pea. Note calyx is turned down, away from the flower.

10 To make a tendril – roll paste into a tiny ball.

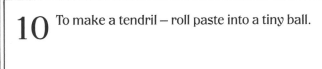

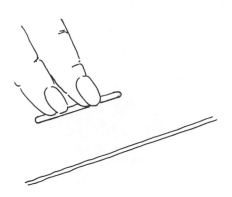

11 Now roll the ball into a long piece of 'rope', either in the palm of your hands or on your work top surface.

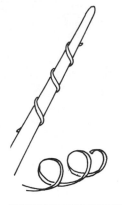

12 Wrap tendril around the back of a paint brush to form curl and simply ease off the brush. Alternatively, simply roll florist tape in your hands and twist tape as above.

13 To make a bud, follow first steps, allowing middle petal to lightly close over first petal. Add calyx.

14 Finished spray.

Alternative cutters.

B62

B61

Note: Leaves do not grow on the same stem as a sweet pea.
Make several blooms in the same colour and a bud or two, and tape together into a spray.

L 117

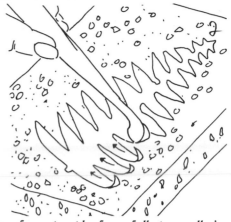

1 Lightly grease worktop surface.
Roll out paste thinly on board and, using cutter No. L11, cut out leaf by applying even pressure over entire surface of cutter.

Remove surplus flower paste and place in plastic bag.

2 Transfer cut out leaf carefully to small piece of foam sponge.

Using Tool No. 3B, gently work fronds. Pull tool from outside edge towards centre. Petals will automatically curl inwards.

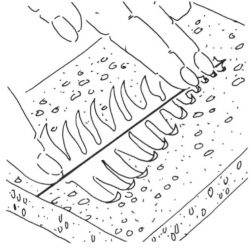

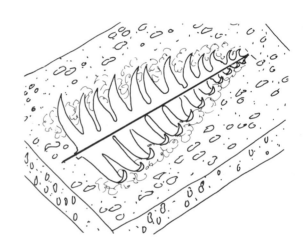

3 Tape a piece of fine florist wire with brown florist tape. Place gum glue over sufficient wire to fit the length of the leaf.

Gently place stem down centre of fern.

4 If necessary, support shape of petals with a small amount of 'cloud'.

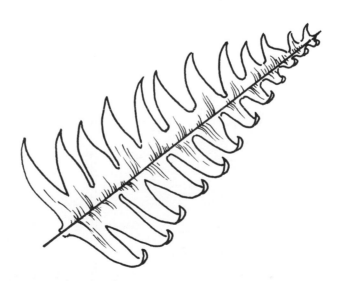

5 Finished leaf.

Alstroemeria

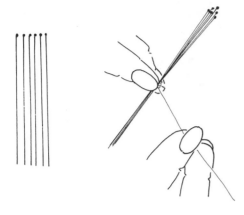

1 Join six fine stamens together using fine fusewire. One stamen, the pistil, must be slightly higher than the other five stamens.

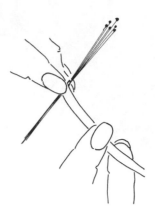

2 Using half width florist tape, tape stamens together securely.

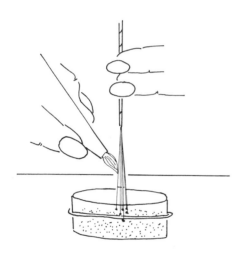

3 Using a paint brush and pink non-toxic chalk, shade stems of stamens.

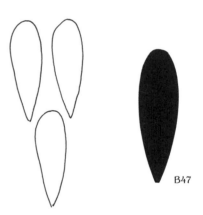

B47

4 Using Cutter No B47 and white paste, cut out three petals.

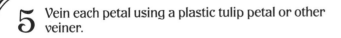

5 Vein each petal using a plastic tulip petal or other veiner.

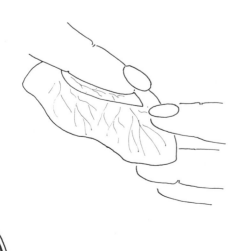

6 Make the necessary markings in a deep mauve colour using a Koki or a paint brush.

7 Pinch the rounded top of the petal between two fingers, creating a pointed effect at the top of the petal. The crease will be towards the stamens, facing inwards.

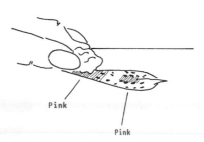

8 Using a small piece of cotton wool or a paint brush, shade the petal pink.

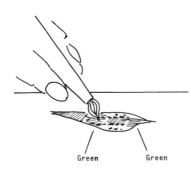

Green   Green

9 Shade the top and middle of the petal green, using a fine brush.

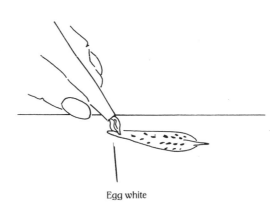

Egg white

10 Use egg white or gum acacia on the base of the petal.

11 Pick up stamens and hang upside down. Place sticky petal against top of stamens.

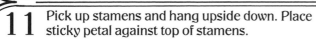

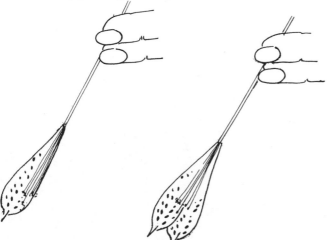

12 Place second petal in position, leaving space for the final inner petal, which should be slightly lower than the first two petals.

13 Now bend the top of the wire over and allow to hang downwards. Support on Handy Holder.

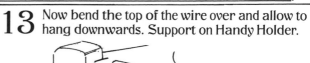

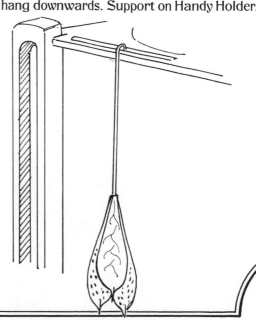

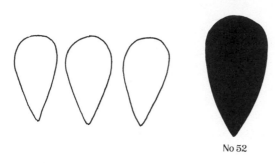

No 52

14 Using Cutter No 52, cut a further three petals.

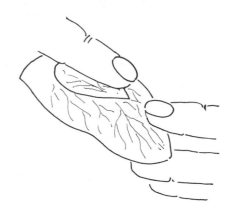

15 Press against vein mould.

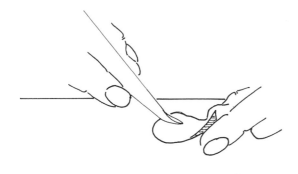

16 Using Tool 4A, gently soften the edges.

17 Place fingers under the top rounded side of the petal and pinch. N.B. This will cause the crease to be in the opposite direction to the first three petals, in that the pointed portion of the crease will be towards the outside of the flower.

18 Using Koki or a fine paint brush, mark the petals in deep maroon as indicated in the sketch.

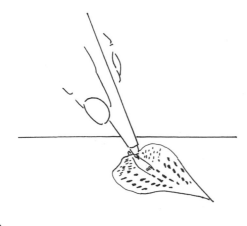

19 Now shade the base of the petal with pale pink chalk.

Pink

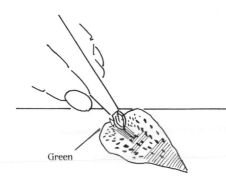

Green

20 Shade the top of the petal light green.

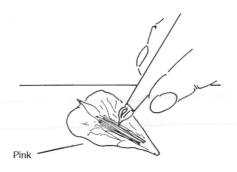

Pink

21 Shade the centre of the petal pink.

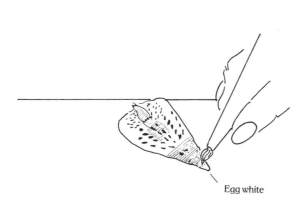

Egg white

22 Place egg white or gum glue at the base of the petal.

23 Attach the petal to the original three petals, placing it between two previous petals.

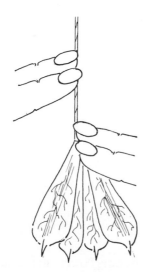

24 Place the next petal on the stem, leaving a space in the centre for the last petal.

25 Add final petal.

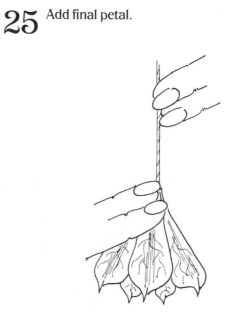

Alstroemeria

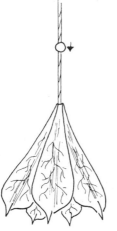

26 Using a tiny ball of green paste, push this down the stem until it meets the petals to form a calyx. A touch of gum glue will help to secure it to the petals.

27 Place your finger-tips over the green ball and cause the paste to form a neat cuplike base for the flower.

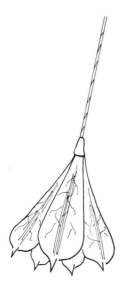

28 The finished calyx.

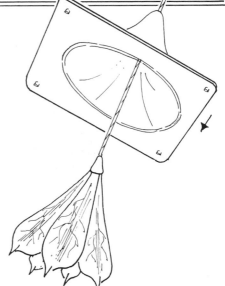

29 Using Flower Support No 4A, place it over the back of the flower and turn it right side up. This will allow the petals to open and dry.

30 Flower from top view.

31 A finished sprig.

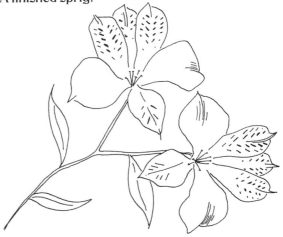

Note: Dry some flowers in the flower support and allow others to hang downwards. This will create the effect of some being more open than others.

ℬauhinia

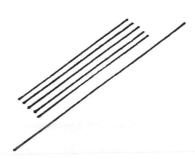

1 Use ready covered white wire (gauge 30) for 5 stamens cut to length. Use a longer length of wire for the pistil.

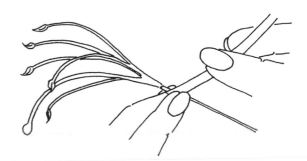

2 Join all the stamens and pistil together with ¼ width green tape. Make anthers out of a little white paste, attach with gum glue.

B 24

3 Cut out 4 petals using Cutter B24, leaving a slightly thicker base for the insertion of wire.

4 Insert wire (gauge 26) into the petals.

5 Using a hibiscus petal veiner, press each petal against veiner.

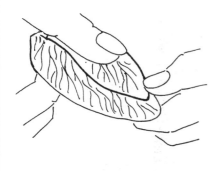

6 Using Tool No. 4A or No. 2B, gently flute edges.

7 Cut out the middle petal slightly thicker than the side petals. Insert wire, vein and widen petal sides by using Tool 4A or Tool 10.

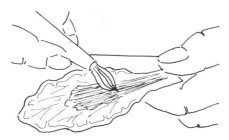

If making the deep mauve bauhinia, shade only the centre petals with a dark maroon/red colour with petal dust. Use a lighter shade for other petals.

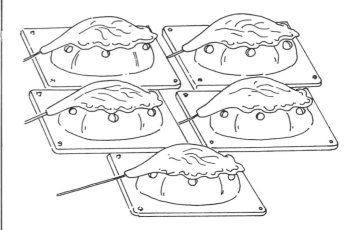

8 Allow the petals to rest on convex shapes or flower supports to dry, if wired; or to partially dry, if no wire is to be used.

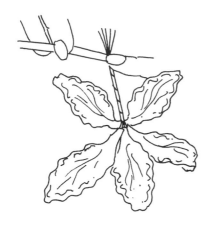

9 When petals are dry, tape together. Two back petals, two side petals and finally the front petal. Make sure the stamens are in the centre of the flower. See sketch 12.

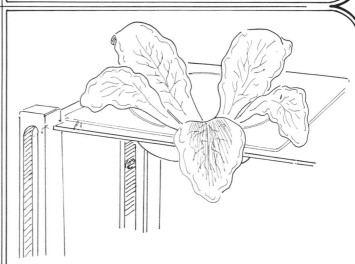

10 If wire has been omitted from the petals, place back right petal in former first, then back left petal. Add front right petal and then front left petal and finally the centre petal. Notice the front petal falls over flower support 1A.

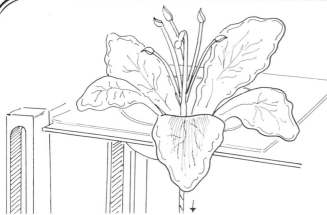

11 Using gum glue placed at the base of the stamens, ease through the centre of the flower. Make sure the stamens bend over the front petal but they occupy the space of an imaginary sixth petal.

12 The finished flower.

Bougainvillaea

L40

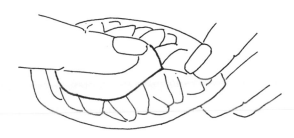

1 Using any suitable shade you like, cut out three petals using Cutter No. L40. Remember to leave a thicker part at the base of the leaf for the insertion of wire. Keep petals under a light cover of plastic to prevent drying out.

2 Vein bract on a rose leaf veiner.

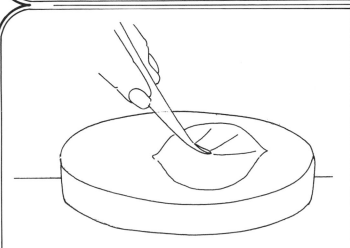

3 Alternatively, using Tool 4B, gently mark in veins, making sure you do not cut the petal. Work on a petal pad.

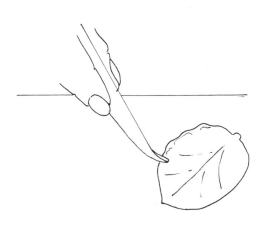

4 Lightly work edges of each petal, either with your fingers or with Tool 4A or Tool 2B so they are slightly fluted.

5 Using thin fuse wire, which bends easily but holds its shape (gauge 30), tape with quarter thickness florist tape. You will need three pieces, each about 5cm (2") long, or a bit longer. Insert wire into bract.

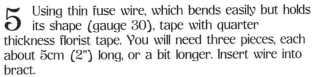

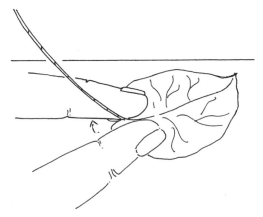

6 Bend base of petal inwards by gently pressing fingers at back of bract lifting the front side of the petal upwards.

7 Use a little cloud to shape petals.

8 Using a stamen with both ends cut off, take a tiny piece of paste the same colour as the petals, and cover the stamen, leaving the tip of the stamen visible. Roll the stamen in the palm of your hand or on the worktop surface.

9 Covered part of stamen should be about 2,5 cm long.

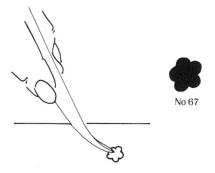

No 67

10 Using Cutter No 67 and yellow paste, cut out tiny flower. Work edges with tool No 4A to create frilly effect.

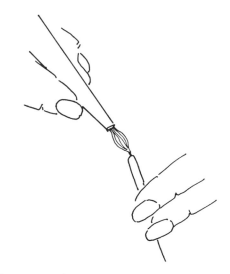

11 Place gum glue on top of stamen.

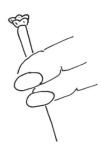

12 Place flower in position. You will need one stamen for each bract, but they do not all have to have a flower on them. Some of these tiny yellow flowers may still be buds, in which case, shape the tip of the stamen in the same colour as the main petals, forming a slight bulge at the top of the stamen.

13 Place a little gum glue at the base of petal - right side up.

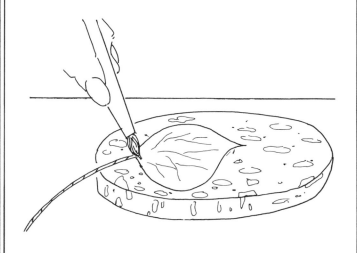

14 Attach stamen to petal. Complete all three petals. Leave to dry. Florist tape may also be used to attach stamen to petal.

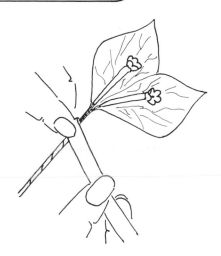

15 Using florist tape, tape the petals together, adding one at a time.

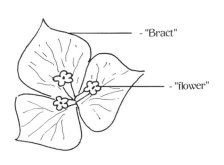

- "Bract"

- "flower"

16 Re-arrange stamens in centre of flower if they have moved out of position.

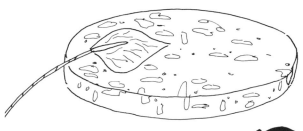

L39

17 Different sized flowers often appear on the same stem, the smaller ones, or buds, at the end of the stem. When using a smaller cutter, Cutter No L39, proceed in the same way as above, but make the stamens smaller, and remember, they will have no little flowers on them.

18 To make the very small closed buds found at the end of the stem, use Cutter No B9 or B18.

B9

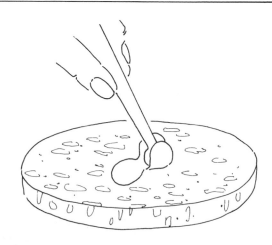

19 Place petal on petal pad, and, from outside of petal, pull Tool 4A towards centre. Vein.

20 Pinch outside edges to give pointed effect.

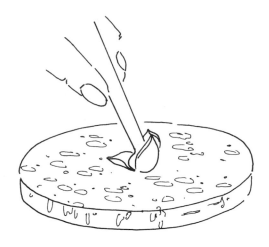

21 Using Tool No 3B, press into the centre to 'cup' flower.

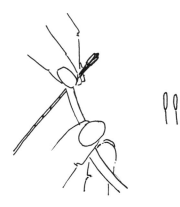

22 Tape three tiny stamens together, the same colour as the flower.

23 Place a little gum glue in the centre of flowers, and gently pull stamens through petals.

24 Small Bougainvillaea flower for end of spray.

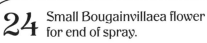

156

Cattleya Orchid

Note: Two methods of constructing this flower are given, with or without the use of wire in each petal. Simply omit all instructions using wire for the unwired orchid. To assemble the wired orchid, *all* petals must be completely dry.

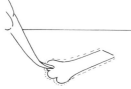

1 Using a firm taped wire (gauge 24), slightly bend the tip into a gentle curve about 5 mm long.

2 Take a small piece of white paste and shape over curved wire. The base will be narrower than the top.

B2

3 Using Cutter No B2, cut out column fairly thickly.

4 Using Tool No 4A, gently work edges of column, slightly increasing it in size.

5 Place egg white or gum glue on shaped stem and cover with column. Make sure that the three small scallops are all neatly arranged, with the centre scallop clearly in the middle.

6 Roll out paste in the colour of your choice not too thinly, and, using Cutter No B1, cut out the slipper. Use Cutter No 54, or similar, to cut out a piece in the centre of the petal.

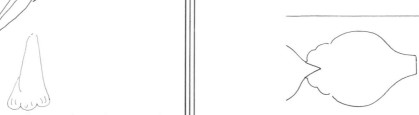

7 Begin working with Tool No 4A from the back of the petal. Place tool in the centre of the petal and work down each side pulling the paste gently in the direction indicated.

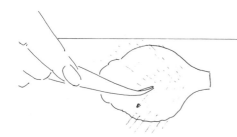

B1

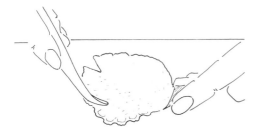

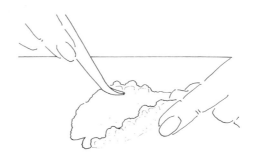

8 Return to back of petal, and, holding the back of the petal in your left hand, begin to encourage petal to flute by gently working Tool 4A over the edges of the petal. Remember to lift the petal after two or three strokes. This lifting of the paste will allow it to have room to stretch, causing an attractive frilled petal.

9 Complete both sides of the petal evenly, ensuring that the centre is adequately frilled.

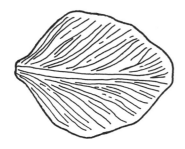

10 Orchid veiner.

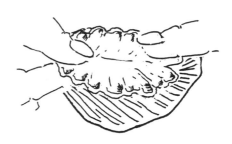

11 Press petal against orchid veiner. Make sure the centre of the petal corresponds with the centre of the mould.

12 If necessary, using Tool 4A, again flute edges ensuring they have not lost their frilly look.

13 Flute both sides of slipper.

14 Shade the slipper with petal dust before placing the column in position.

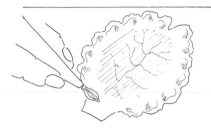

15 Place a little egg white or gum glue at the base of the petal.

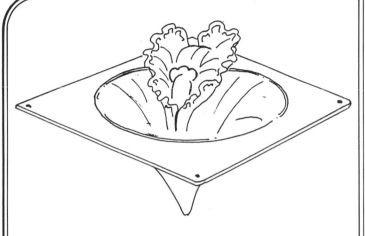

16 Attach the completed column to the centre. Lift up the sides of the petal, making sure that they meet evenly above the column - see illustration. Now ease the orchid slipper into flower former 4A and allow it to completely dry.

17 Using Cutters Nos B13 and B14, roll out paste with a thicker base (to allow for the insertion of fine, taped, hooked wire). Cut one of each, making sure you do not turn petals upside down, or you will muddle them.

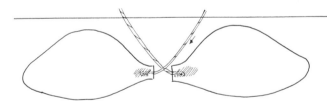

18 In the same way as for the slipper, vein the two side petals.

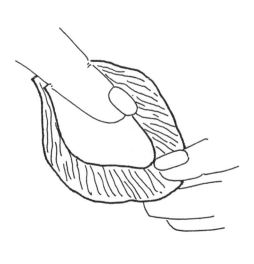

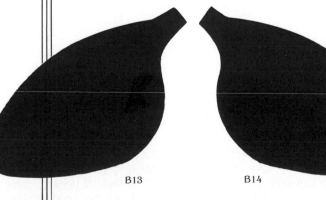

B13   B14

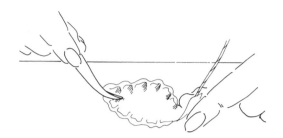

19 Using Tool 4A or 2B, work the edges of the petal, causing it to frill. Frill both side petals.

20 Using Cutter No B4, cut three petals with a thick base (for the insertion of fine, taped, hooked wire).

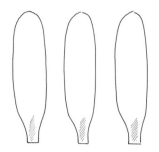

Wired sepal.

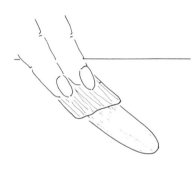

21 Using a corn leaf veiner, press veins into each sepal. Pick up each sepal in fingers and gently work fingers around sepal causing the edges to soften. Ends of sepals should have a slightly pointed effect.

B4

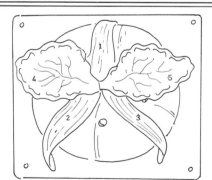

22 If you have not used wire, use flower support 1A in the convex position to assemble orchid. Clip it on to the Handy Holder as this will prevent the flower from slipping and sliding. Place one sepal in the centre over a small flat piece of paste forming a base. Place the next two sepals on the opposite sides of the flower support, forming an upside-down "Y" shape. Use gum glue to hold sepals in position. Place the two side petals in position, using gum glue to secure.

23 Place gum glue in the centre of the orchid supported on the convex flower support.

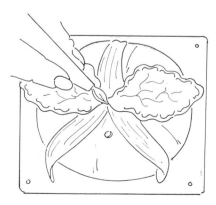

24 Carefully ease dry slipper into position. Prop up petals with a little 'cloud' until dry.

25 To assemble wired orchid, begin with the side petals. Use tape to hold them in position.

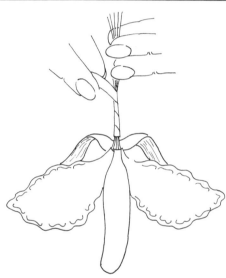

26 Tape the three lateral sepals in position. Hold petals upside-down to ensure that the sepals are evenly and correctly positioned.

27 Finally, ease slipper into position. Tape to secure. Finished orchid.

28 Alternative Cutters to make a Cattleya orchid.

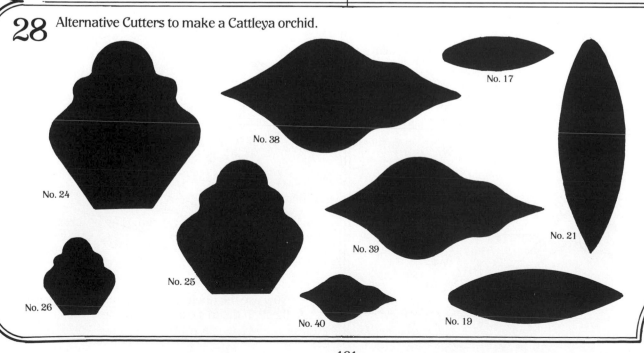

No. 17

No. 38

No. 21

No. 24

No. 39

No. 25

No. 26

No. 40

No. 19

Chrysanthemum

1 Use a fairly firm taped wire, gauge 24. Make a flat hook at the top.

B 37

2 Cut out one petal using Cutter No. B37.

B 36

3 Cut two petals using No. B36 Cutter. Using sharp knife, split each petal.

4 Using egg white, or gum glue, and a paint brush, tip the centre of each petal with the glue.

5 Place the three layers of petals one on top of the other, allowing the petals to fall in between each other.

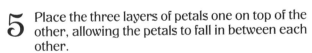

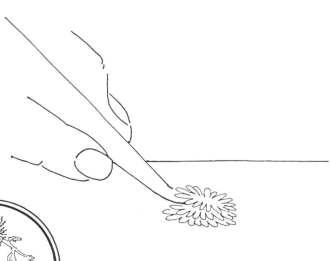

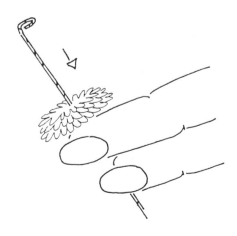

6 Now use the hooked taped wire and gently ease through the three layers of paste.

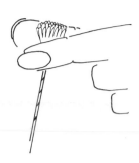

7 Lift up the sides of the petals creating the centre of the flower. If petals do not stay together, allow centre to hang down on the flower support of handy holder.

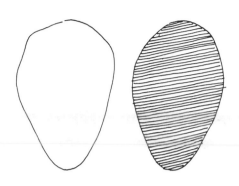

8 Now use two shades of paste – the darker shade is the colour you will see on the inside of the flower; the pale shade is the back of the petal.

9 Place the dark shade over the light shade of flower paste.

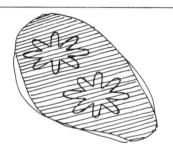

B 35

10 Using cutter No. B35, cut out three petals.

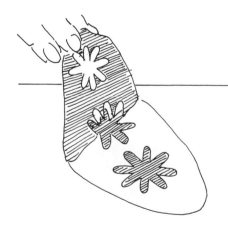

11 Lift the dark shade off the light shade and return it to a plastic bag. Return the light shade to another plastic bag.

12 Split petals.

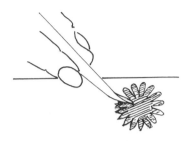

13 Using tool No. 4A, press down on each cut petal, causing the petal to fan out with a slightly pointed tip. Using a paint brush, tip centre with egg white or gum glue.

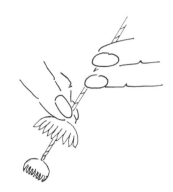

14 Push wire through centre petal and lift up to centre of flower. Hold centre downwards.

15 Hold centre upside down and join next two petals to the centre of flower.

B 34

16 Cut out two petals using Cutter No. B34. Lift separate colours as shown in step 11.

Place petals on foam and using tool No. 4A, press each petal from outside towards inside, causing the petals to curl inwards.

17 Make sure the tips of the petals are slightly pointed by gently pressing the petals between index finger and thumb.

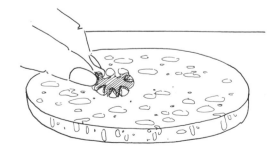

18 Using a paint brush, tip centre with egg white or gum glue.

19 Continue to build up flower.

20 Holding flower support No. 5A upside-down, place stem through support.

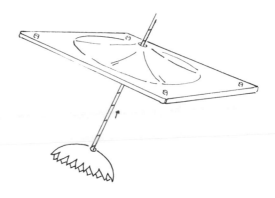

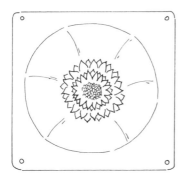

21 Turn flower support right side up and allow petals to rest as you proceed.

22 Cut two petals using Cutter No. B33 and proceed as before, remembering to make sure petals have a pointed tip.

23 Cut two petals using Cutter No. B32.

B
32

B
33

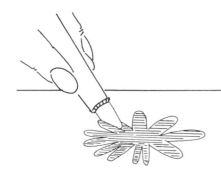

24 Split each petal with sharp knife.

25 Place petals on foam, and, using tool No. 4A, work petals from the outside inwards causing petals to curl inwards.

26 Continue to build up flower.

27 Cut out two more petals using Cutter No. B32.

28 Cut each petal in half, splitting all the petals as before.

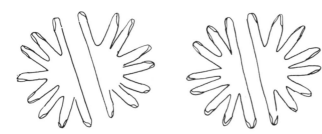

29 Place petals on the back of the flower as illustrated.

30 Place the next two petals across the first two. To increase the size of your chrysanthemum still further, use cutters 18 and 19. Mark and curl (see Page 12). Add as many petals as required.

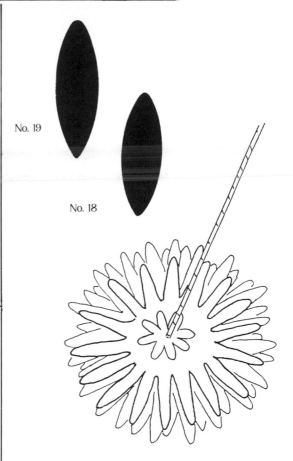

No. 19

No. 18

31 Using green paste and Cutter No. 35, cut out calyx.
Place calyx at the back of the flower. Return flower to support and allow to dry.

32 Finished flower.

Chrysanthemum Leaves

Note: There are two ways to stem leaves. You may either ease the wire into the flower paste which has been rolled out slightly thicker at the base to hold the wire; or you may simply attach the wire to the back of the leaf using gum glue.

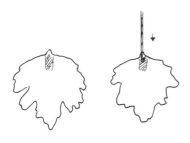

L22

L25

B56

1 Using white flower paste, cut out leaves using Cutter Nos B56, or L22 and L25. Remember to roll out paste carefully, allowing for the insertion of the wire should you choose this method. If you are going to insert a fine, taped, hooked wire into the leaf, do it now. Make sure that the wire is not visible on either side of the leaf. Secure with a touch of egg white on stem.

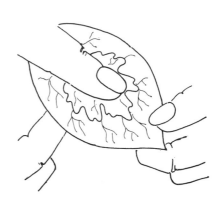

2 Press leaf against leaf veiner.

3 Alternatively, use a fine wire which has been taped and curved into the position you wish to use for the support of the leaf.

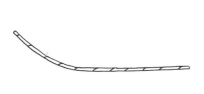

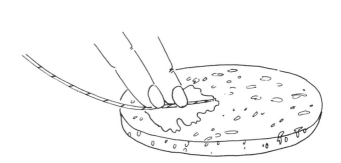

4 Apply gum glue to wire over the length of the leaf it is to be attached to.

5 When leaves are dry, shade them with non-toxic chalks. Use a dark blue/green colour and shade both sides of leaf. Use a yellow chalk on the outside edges on the top of the leaf.

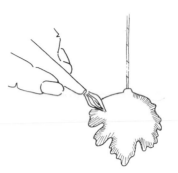

6 Using a cooking spray, lightly and evenly spray both sides of leaves. This will give the leaf 'life' and a natural sheen will remain. If you do not have a cooking spray, hold the leaves in the steam of a boiling kettle for a few seconds. This will also create a life-like effect.

7 Finished sprig.

Note: All leaves can be made using these methods. The secret is in the shading of the leaves – experiment with many colours. Work from real leaves wherever possible.

Clivia

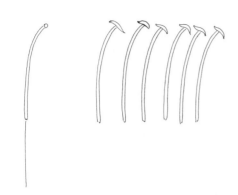

1 Use covered white wire (gauge 30) shaded yellow for the six stamens and the pistil. Make the anthers out of a little paste, attach to wire with a little gum glue. The pistil has a tiny round head.

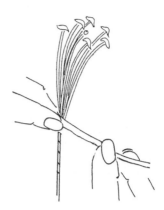

2 Using quarter width florist tape, tape stamens to pistil. Space stamens evenly with pistil in the centre.

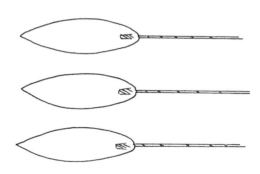

3 Cut out three petals using yellow paste and Cutter No. 21. Remember to allow a thicker base for wire insertion.

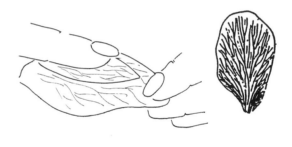

4 Press each petal against a hibiscus veiner.

5 Using orange petal dust and a bit of cotton wool, colour petals orange, leaving the base of the petal yellow. (about a quarter of the petal).

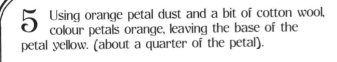

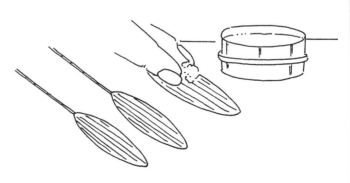

6 Move petals to clean surface. Now colour back of the petals completely with the orange petal dust.

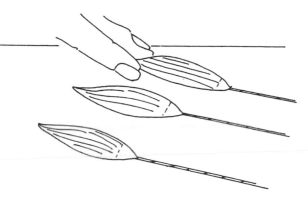

7 Using thumb and index finger, gently crease petals outwards on the front side which shows the yellow base.

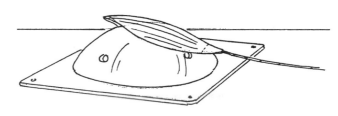

8 Allow petals to dry over convex surface. Flower former 1A.

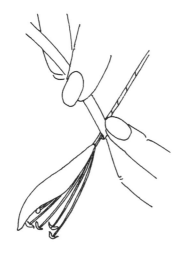

9 Tape petals to stamens using quarter width tape.

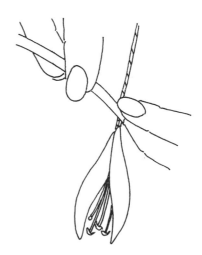

10 Make sure the first row of three petals is evenly spaced when taped together.

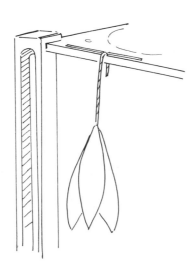

11 Hang petals over side of Handy Holder.

12 The next three petals could be left without wire and attached to the stem when partially dry using a little gum glue; or if preferred may be cut out, wired and dried in the same way as the first row. In which case they will be taped to the stem.

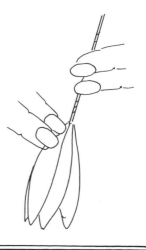

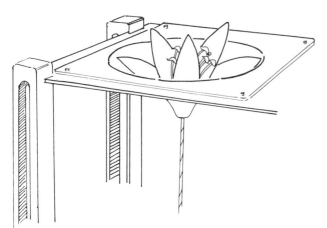

13 If outside petals have been attached with gum glue, it will be necessary to support petals in flower support 4A.

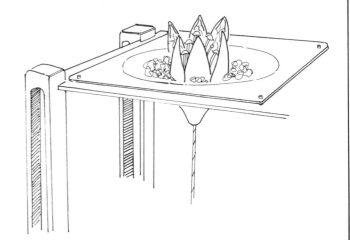

14 Use some 'cloud' to support the petals in an upward position.

15 Single flower.

16 Clivia and bud.

Note: Clivia does not grow on individual stems but in a cluster on a main stem.

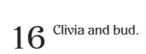

Disa

1 Tape two fine wires and bend.

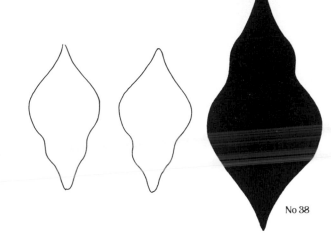

2 Using Cutter No 38, cut two petals. A pale pink paste should be used.

No 38

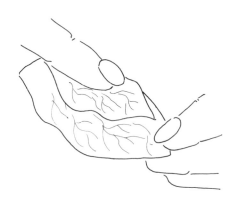

3 Using veiner, or plastic tulip petal, press cut out petals to vein.

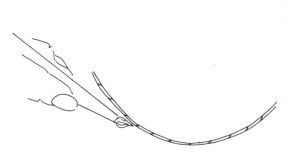

4 Paint taped wire with gum glue to equal the length of the petal.

5 Turn petals upside down (no veins showing) and press gummed curved wire into centre of petal and allow paste to adhere. Dry completely.

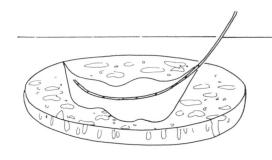

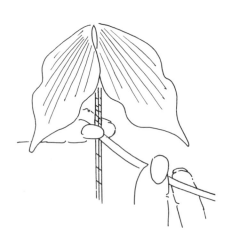

6 Join wires together with half width of tape.

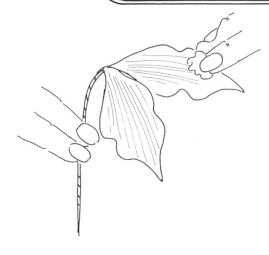

7 Shade with a deep tomato pink non-toxic chalk and set aside. (Use cotton wool).

8 Roll a piece of pale yellow paste into a ball slightly larger than a marble.

9 Shape the ball into a 'Mexican hat'. Slightly bend the top of the 'hat'.

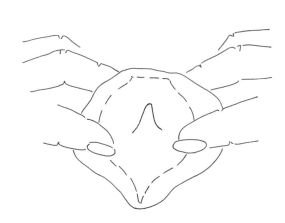

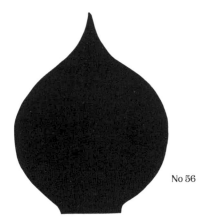

No 56

10 Now using Cutter No 56, hold cutter in left hand; place paste over cutter, ensuring that 'tail' is in the centre of the cutter and the pointed part is leaning towards the base of the petal. Ease fingers around the cutter, causing the cutter to cut the paste. Return surplus paste to plastic bag.

12 Allow 'tail' part of petal to fall between your index finger and middle finger. Using tool No. 3B, gently hollow out petal, ensuring sides are curled inwards.

11 Separate cutter from paste by gently easing apart.

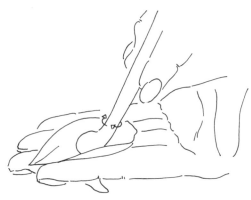

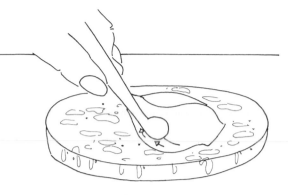

13 Place petal on foam, and gently work Tool 3B down both sides of petal creating a deeper cupping effect.

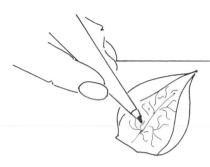

14 Using a red felt tip pen, or a fine paint brush, draw in lines to indicate veins in back petal.

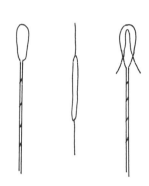

15 Using taped wire, cover the tip with white paste in a tear drop shape. Using a stamen and a tiny piece of paste, cover the middle of the stamen with paste as illustrated. Place this over the tear drop on the wire.

No 29

No 54

16 Using Cutter No 29 and a pale shade of yellow paste, cut out petal. Use same cutter or Cutter No 54 to cut out a small piece of petal to form 'heart shape'.

17 Place petal on foam, and, using Tool 3B, hollow out.

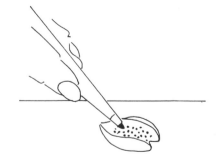

18 Using felt tip pen or paint brush, paint in tiny red dots all over the centre of this petal.

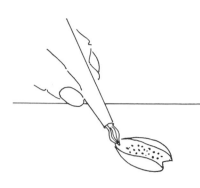

19 At pointed base of petal apply gum glue.

20 Place petal at the back of paste on wire.

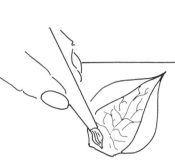

21 Now apply gum glue to base of larger petal.

22 Place centre of flower into back petal, allowing the centre to sit on the inside of the petal (allow petal to curl forward to support middle). Leave to dry completely.

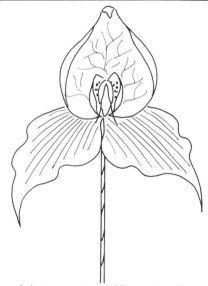

23 Now join top centre of flower to the two lower petals of the flower. Tape stems together using half width tape.

25 Place in position over the gap in the two side petals of the disa.
Finished flower. (Note: The disa belongs to the orchid family and can be found growing wild in the S.W. Cape).

No 16

24 Using cutter No 16, cut one. Make three minute little white 'balls' and attach to top of "tongue".

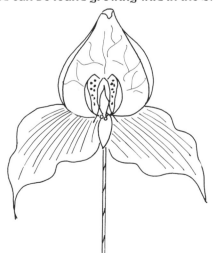

1 Tape a piece of firm wire (gauge 24) and cover the tip with a small piece of paste. This will be used as a base on which to stick the petals.

B 68

2 Using cutter No. B68, cut three petals. Cover the petals not in use with soft plastic, or a plastic lid, to prevent drying.

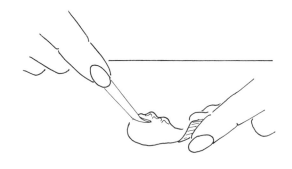

3 Using tool No. 2B, or tool No. 4A, gently flute the rounded edges of each of the three petals.

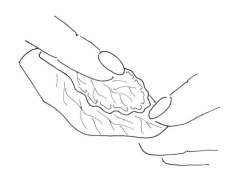

4 Press each petal against a plastic tulip petal or other suitable veiner to create realistic veins on the petals.

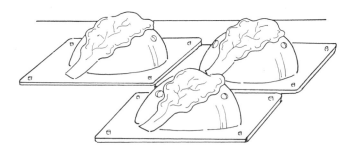

5 Place each petal over a half ping-pong ball, or similar shape, and allow to partially dry.

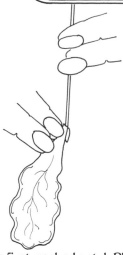

6 Begin with the first worked petal. Place a little egg white or gum glue on the inside of the petal and gently attach it to the covered wire.

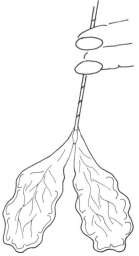

7 Add the second petal, spaced evenly apart to allow the third petal to fit in its position.

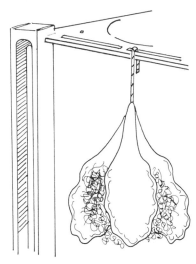

8 Place the third petal in position and then gently place a ball of 'cloud' in the centre of the petals, allowing them to dry evenly.

B68

9 Now cut out three more petals using the same cutter, Cutter No. B68.

Using the same tool as before, gently flute the edges of each petal.

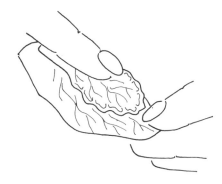

10 Press the petals against the veiner.

11 Cut out a further three petals using cutter No. B67.

B 67

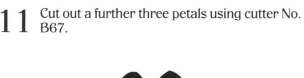

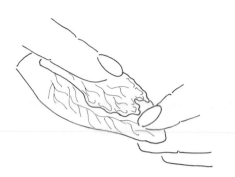

12 Press the petals against a veiner.

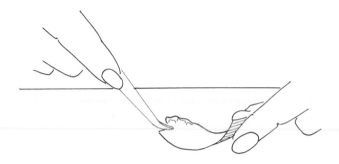

13 Using Tool 2B or 4A, gently flute the edges as for previous petals.

14 Place the petals on soft foam, and, using Tool 4A, gently pull the tool from the top of the petal to the base, creating a ridge-like effect, which must be uppermost on the petal.

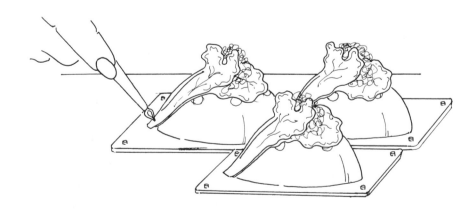

15 Using a little egg white or gum glue, join the base of the petal from Cutter No. B67 to the one made with Cutter No. B68. Cutter No. B67 is uppermost. Using a tiny piece of 'cloud' to lift outside petal up, gently place between petals.

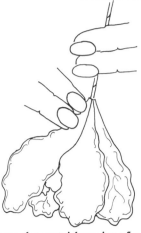

16 Pick up the outside pairs of petals one at a time, and placing a little gum glue on the top of the base, place one petal between the first and second petal of the now dried previous layer.

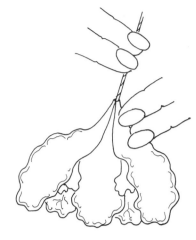

17 Now place each remaining pair of petals between the second and third petals. Note that the petals are held in a downward position.

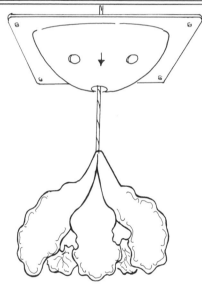

18 Using Flower Support No. 5B in the convex position, gently ease petals through the hole in the support.

19 Clip flower support to Handy Holder stand and gently place small tufts of 'cloud' under petals to slightly raise the outside petals.

20 Finished Flower.

Note: When the flower is dry, shade petals with chalk. If you have a white Dutch iris, use yellow chalk on the lowest petal just under petal No. 67.

To neaten the stem, allow flower to completely dry and then cut thin strips of green paste, tapering them slightly, and ease them over the petal joins. The Dutch iris does not have a visible calyx. The green should be a light greyish green.

1 Cut five stamens into approximately ⅓ of their length. Using a minute amount of yellow paste, cover tips.

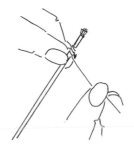

2 Using a fairly firm wire (gauge No 24) for main stem, secure stamens to stem with fine fuse wire.

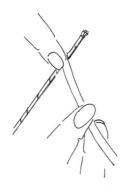

3 Cover wire with ½ width florist tape to neaten.

4 Lightly tip the tips of the stamens with egg white or gum glue.

5 Carefully dip the tips of the stamens into coloured pollen (usually red). The pollen could be maize meal or colourless gelatin shaded with non-toxic red chalk.

6 Using paste a shade lighter than the petals, form a longish thin sausage. Hold the stem in your hand and place the 'sausage' on the stem.

181

*H*ibiscus

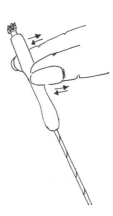

7 Now work paste on the wire by evenly rolling backwards and forwards over wire. In order to ensure that the paste 'grips' the wire, you may need to apply a little pressure to the paste and wire.

8 The base of the stem is wider than the middle part. The top part of the pistil needs to be thicker than it is in the actual flower as we have to have something on which to support the many little stamens.

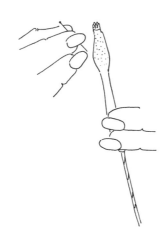

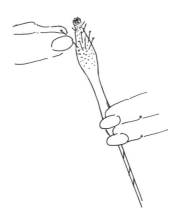

9 Using a pin, prick a number of holes into the top part of the pistil.

10 Have numerous bits of stamen cut (without heads) and place these pieces of stamen into the holes.
If you battle to do this with your fingers, you may find tweezers useful.

12 Tip the edges of these stamens with egg white or gum glue. Then, using a dry paint brush, dust
yellow pollen over the stamens.

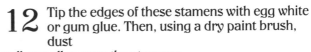

11 Place as many stamens into the pistil as possible.

B39

13 Cut out five petals using cutter B39. Cover petals with soft plastic or a plastic lid to prevent drying of petals.

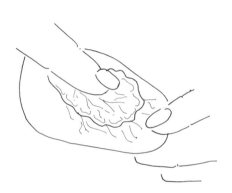

14 Mark in veins, using a plastic tulip petal or other veiner.

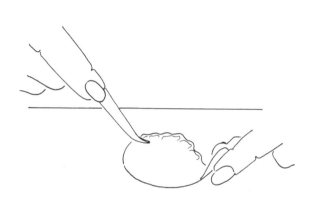

15 Using tool 2B or 4A, flute the edges of the petals.

16 Place petals over half a ping-pong ball or similar shape as you proceed.

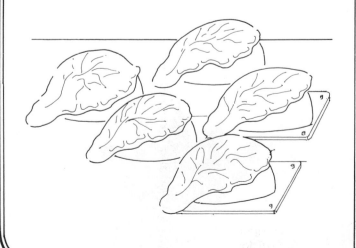

17 Using flower support No 4A, clip on to Handy Holder stand. Lightly grease with white vegetable fat, and place first petal in position as illustrated. Add egg white or gum glue to base of first petal.

18 Add additional petals, allowing them to slightly overlap each other.

19 Make sure the five petals are evenly spaced.

20 Shade centre of flower, if desired, when glue is dry.

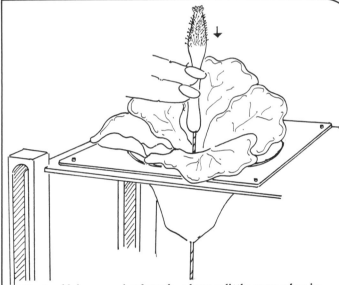

21 Using a paint brush, place a little gum glue in the centre of flower. Now place pistil in position, easing wire through hole in flower support.

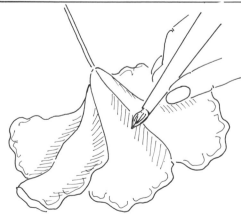

22 When flower is dry, use non-toxic chalk to shade back of petals as illustrated. Use a darker shade than the paste you have used.

23 Cut out calyx using cutter B38.

B38

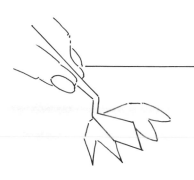

24 Using artist's palette knife, flatten each sepal to increase its size.

25 Place egg white or gum glue on the sepals and carefully position the calyx over the back of the flower, ensuring that it covers any untidy join the flower may have.

No. 23

26 Now using Cutter No 23 or B55, cut out the 'double' calyx this flower has.

27 Join second calyx to flower. In a real flower, this little 'calyx' stands away from the rest of the flower.

28 A finished flower.

*I*ris

1 Using a firm wire (gauge 24), tape and cover tip with a tiny piece of flower paste on which to stick the petals of the flower.

2 Using Cutter No. B65, cut out three petals. Cover with soft plastic or a plastic lid to prevent petals from drying out.

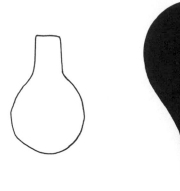

B65

3 Using tool 2B or tool 4A, gently flute the outside edges of the petals.

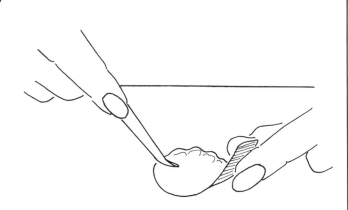

4 Press petal against plastic tulip petal or other veiner, wet side down, to form veins. If fluting is damaged, reflute edges. The wet side is the side of the paste that was touching your worktop surface.

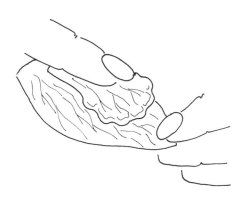

5 Place formed petals over half a ping-pong ball or flower formers to semi-dry.

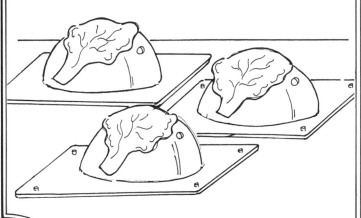

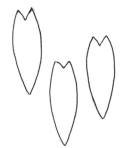

B66

6 Now using cutter No. B66, cut three more petals. Cover with soft plastic or lid.

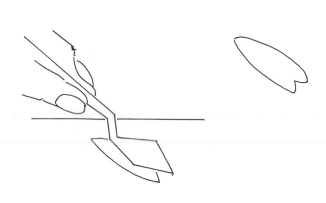

7 Using an artist's palette-knife, flatten each petal to increase it in size.

8 Place this petal on some foam, and, using Tool 4A, gently pull the tool down the centre, causing a crease to form down the middle of it. The crease must be uppermost on the side of the petals which will show in the flower.

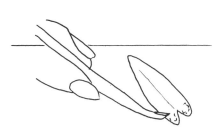

9 Gently flute the edges of this petal, causing it to frill slightly.

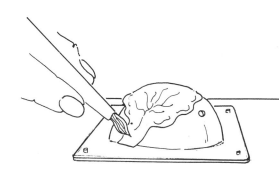

10 Using a little egg white or gum glue, secure B66 to B65, making sure ridge of B66 is uppermost.

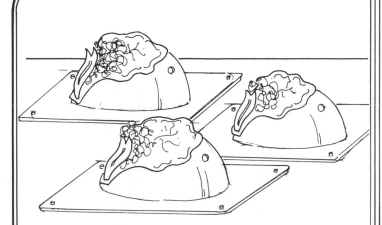

11 Place a little bit of 'cloud' between the petals, causing the small petal to stand away from the larger one.

12 Using egg white or gum glue, attach petals to stem, with the smaller petals towards the centre.

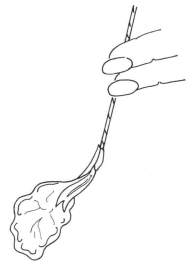

Iris

13 Attach all three petals, holding the flower upside down.

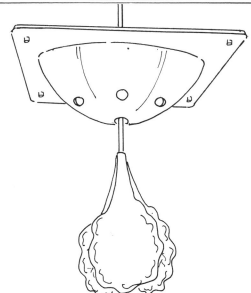

14 Now using flower support No. 5B, place support over petals in the convex position.

15 Place support on Handy Holder stand and allow petals to completely dry in the illustrated position.

16 Using a piece of wire mesh or a strainer, gently force some paste through the sieve.

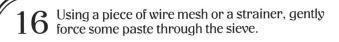

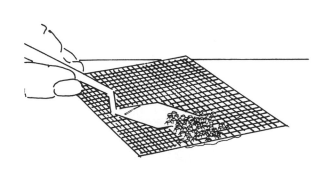

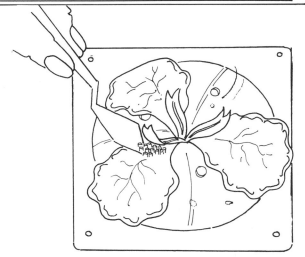

17 Place a little egg white in a straight line under the small petal. Pick up the bits with a palette-knife and place on petals. Be careful to ensure that the pollen fits under the small petal, and that it is carefully placed in a straight line.

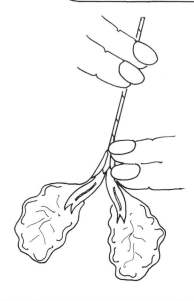

Iris

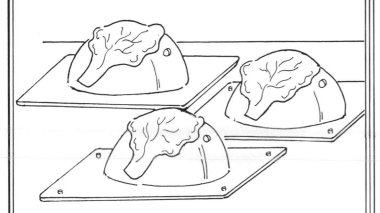

18 Now cut three more petals, using Cutter B65. Flute and vein as before, resting petals on ping-pong balls or similar shapes to partially dry.

19 Now place petals on foam, and, using Tool 4A, gently ease over petal, beginning at top of petal and moving towards base, causing petal to curve in slightly. The ridge must appear on the outside of the petal when joining it to the rest of the flower.

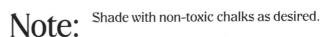

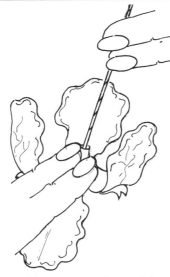

20 Use egg white or gum glue to join to other petals. Hold stem upside-down, and add each petal between previous row of petals.

Note: Shade with non-toxic chalks as desired.

22 When completely dry, turn flower right-side up and remove 'cloud'. To neaten stem of flower, long thin grey/green leaves may be placed over joins. There is no visible calyx on this flower.

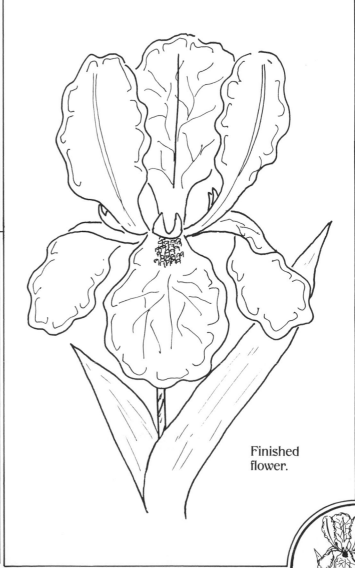

Finished flower.

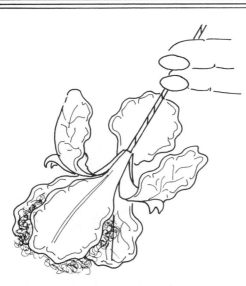

21 When all three petals have been added, place a small ball of 'cloud' into the centre of the flower to form the rounded top. Dry flower upside-down.

No 72

1 Roll paste into a ball a bit larger than a marble. Shape into 'Mexican hat'. Make sure edges are wide enough to fit over Cutter No 72.

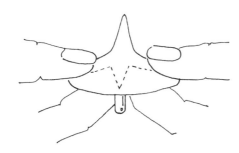

2 Holding Cutter No 72 in your left hand, place the 'Mexican hat' over the middle of the cutter. Begin to press paste against cutting edge. Remove surplus paste to plastic bag.

3 Using Tool 2B, open throat of sepals to form a fairly deep cavity in which to place the petals.

4 Now using Tool 4A, slightly flatten edges of sepals. Neaten with scissors if necessary. Use Tool 6a to 'cup' the centre of the sepals.

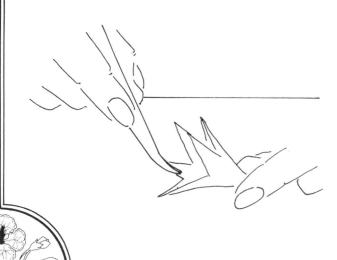

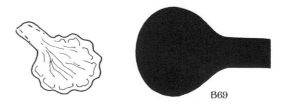

B69

5 Cut out five petals using Cutter No B69. Trim side edges slightly. Place under soft plastic to prevent drying out.

Nasturtium

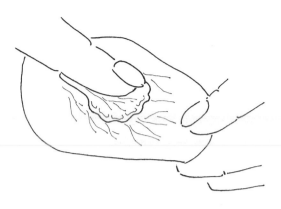

6 Press petals against plastic tulip leaf or other veiner.

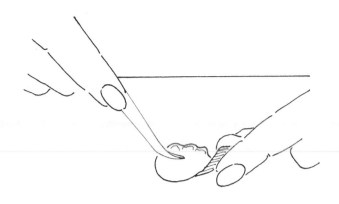

7 Using Tool No 2B or 4A, flute edges of petals until soft and frilly.

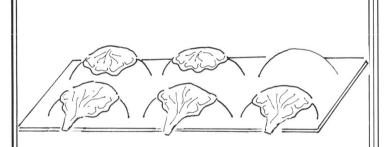

8 Place petals over back of artist's palette to partially dry.

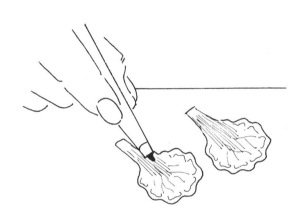

9 Using a paint brush and non-toxic water colours or a koki pen, shade two petals in a darker colour.

11 Place the two shaded petals in position on the sepals. These two petals will form the back petals on the calyx.

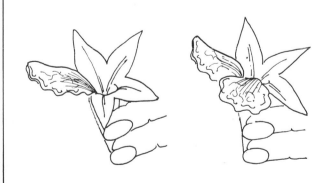

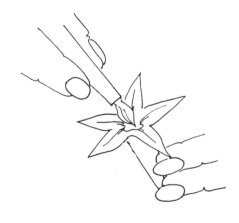

10 Apply egg white or gum glue to the sepals.

Nasturtium

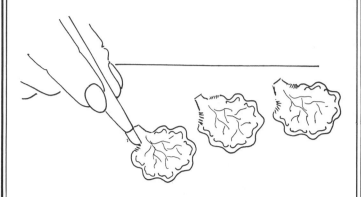

12 Using a sharp craft knife, cut small incisions into the base of the sides of the three remaining petals. Lift up these little edges so they stand upright.

13 Apply egg white or gum glue to sepals and place a petal on either side of the two shaded petals.

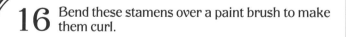

14 Place the final petal in position, allowing it to rest slightly forward of the two side petals. Rest in small hole in Handy Holder.

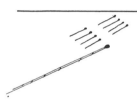

15 Cut eight tiny stamens, with small heads. Tape a fine wire (gauge 26). This will be the pistil.

16 Bend these stamens over a paint brush to make them curl.

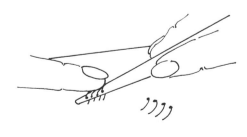

17 Tape stamens to the stem. Keep one stamen away from the others.

18 Place a little gum glue into the centre of the flower and carefully insert the stamens into the flower. The stamens should be bending towards the back shaded petals. The wire should penetrate the side of the calyx.

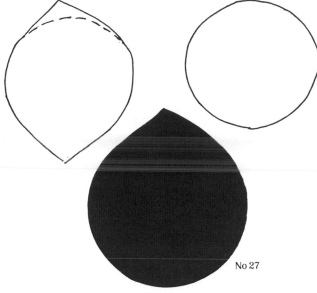

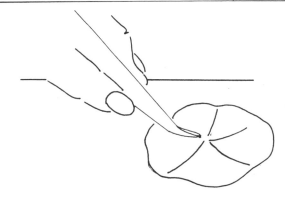

No 27

19 The leaf for this flower may be made by using Cutter No 27. When you have cut the leaf out, simply turn the cutter around and cut the petal again, removing the pointed tip of the petal. This forms a circle.

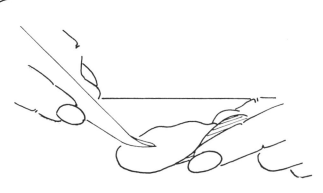

20 Using Tool 4A or 2B, flute the edges of the leaf, causing them to frill slightly.

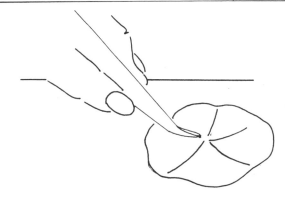

21 Mark in the veins using Tool 4B.

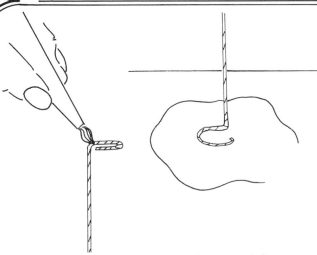

22 To stem the leaf — use a fine, taped, flat hooked, wire to secure to back of leaf with gum glue, *or* the 'Mexican hat' principle may also be used. Ensure the centre of the leaf has sufficient body to hold the wire in the paste.

23 Finished flower.

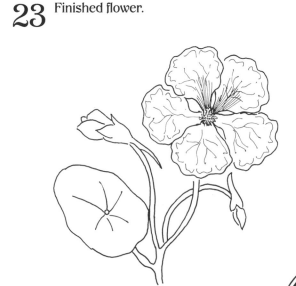

$\mathcal{P}$halaenopsis

1 Tape wire, gauge 26, and bend the wire as illustrated.

2 To make the column, roll a small piece of paste about half the size of a pea into a sausage shape and ease on to the curve in the wire. Mark with non-toxic water colours, or a fine koki pen.

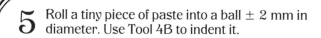

3 Take a tiny piece of paste about one fifth the size of a pea, roll it into a ball and then into a tear-drop shape. Using tool 4A, shape as shown, causing one end to be slightly pointed and the other slightly rounded.

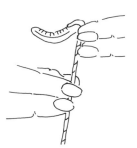

4 To form the column, place the pointed tip over the top of the bend of the wire facing down the long sausage part of the centre.

5 Roll a tiny piece of paste into a ball ± 2 mm in diameter. Use Tool 4B to indent it.

6 Place this "butterfly" on the tip of the wire.

194

$\mathcal{P}$halaenopsis

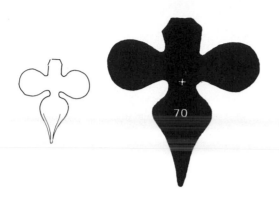

7 Make the lip using Cutter No. 70. Roll out paste and using a sharp knife, make two incisions in the lip.

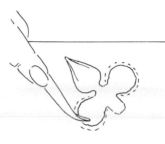

8 Using Tool No. 4A or 2B, work edges of each side of rounded shape to increase the size, and thin the edges.

9 Place the lip on a petal pad and using Tool 3A, gently cup each side. Also using this tool, ease it gently up and down over the centre part of the lip.

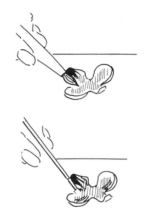

10 Having shaped the lip of the orchid, now shade it with petal dust, first using a paint brush, and then use a cocktail stick to make the dots. Mix a little dust in a drop of gin for this purpose.

12 Carefully attach the lip to the wire, ensuring that the back of the centre of the lip is attached to the top of the bent wire. Place this into a suitable base to dry, e.g. an artist's plastic palette or flower support 3B. A little 'cloud' might be necessary to support the lip of the orchid.

11 Using a paint brush, carefully place gum glue under the column.

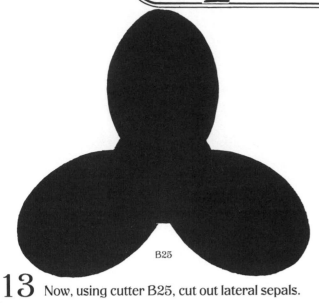

B25

13 Now, using cutter B25, cut out lateral sepals.

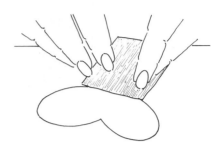

14 Using a corn leaf veiner, lightly mark each sepal - make sure the markings are running vertically with the petal, i.e. from the centre outwards.

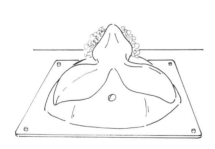

15 Place lateral sepals on flower support 1A in the convex position. Prop up dorsal sepal (back sepal) with a little 'cloud'.

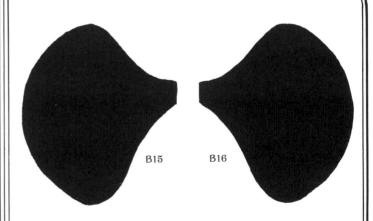

B15   B16

16 Now using Cutters No. B15 and B16, cut out the side petals.

17 Lightly vein with the corn leaf veiner. Work edges with Tool 2B or 4A. Soften edges between fingers and lightly crease the petals down the centre of each petal, see step 19.

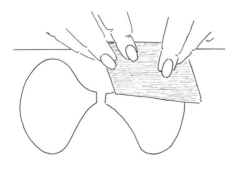

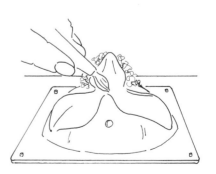

18 Place a little gum glue in the centre of the sepals.

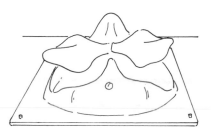

19 Place the side petals in position on each side of the dorsal sepal. Allow them to rest on top of the front lateral sepals.

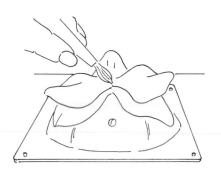

20 Place gum glue in centre of flower.

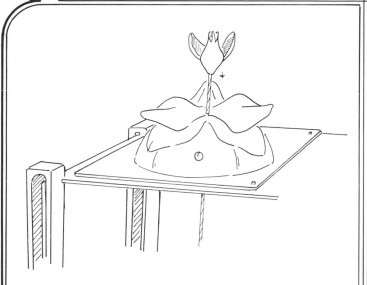

21 Ease dry lip into position, ensuring that the pointed tips are facing the front of the flower.

22 Finished moth orchid.

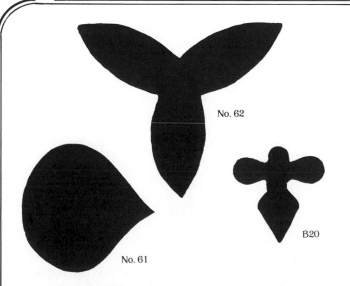

No. 62

No. 61

B20

Note: Alternative Cutters for Moth Orchid: No. 62, No. 61 and No. B20.

Note: There are many shapes and sizes of this flower. They come in a variety of colours. Try to work from a real flower, or a good illustration.

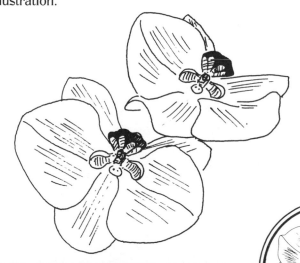

Tea Rose

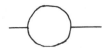

1 Roll out a ball of paste a bit larger than a marble. The size of the ball will depend on the size of the rose you wish to make.

2 Flatten the top half of the ball using your fingers.

3 Use a roller and roll out the top half of the ball thinly, working from the bulge to the outside edge.

WET SIDE

DRY SIDE

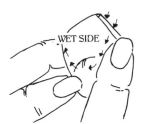

WET SIDE

4 Pick up the paste, with the wet side facing you. (The wet side is the side which was on the greased worktop surface).

5 Now, with the wet side facing you, roll the paste tightly, working from the top right hand corner, down over the bulge, and up the other side.

6 It is important that a tightly closed top is formed. Note the progressive steps of the rolled petal being wrapped around the centre cone.

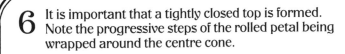

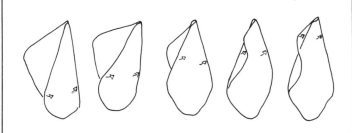

7 The centre should have the last of the rolled petal lying flat against the cone. Do *not* fold this petal back. Insert taped hooked wire, gauge 24 now, or after the addition of some of the centre petals.

8 It may be necessary to remove surplus paste from the base of the rose, depending on the size rose you wish to make. If necessary, remove the surplus paste before inserting wire.

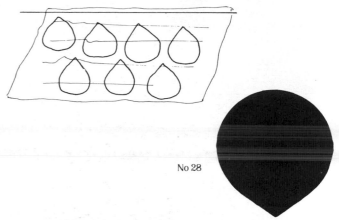

No 28

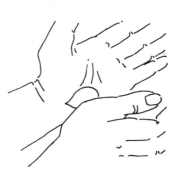

9 Using Cutter No 28 or 29, depending on the size of the bud you have made, roll out a few petals and cover them with soft plastic to prevent drying out.

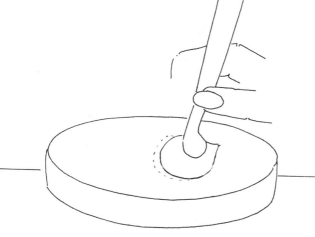

10 Work edges of petals on a petal pad with Tool 3A or Tool 6A. Stretch the petal, making it longer.

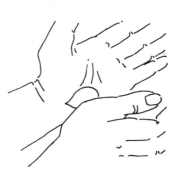

11 Optional - vein the petals between your palms. Or gently roll the petals out between crêpe paper which has been lightly greased with vegetable fat to create veins. It is very important that all the petals have a thin, soft appearance and they should be translucent.

12 Place the first petal over the last fold in the centre which should be lying against the cone. DO NOT bend the top of the petal – it must stand straight upwards against the centre for the rose and should be placed very slightly above the cone.

13 Continue to place petals on the centre of the rose, remembering not to bend the top of the petals. First one petal one way, and then the next petal exactly opposite the previous petal. Continue to do this until you have created a good centre for the rose with a number of petals all standing upright.

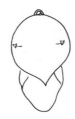

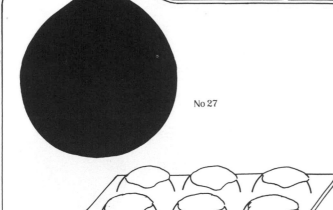

No 27

14 Now, using a slightly larger cutter (Cutter No. 27), depending on the size rose you are making, make more petals, veining as before. Allow them to partially dry over the back of an artist's palette.

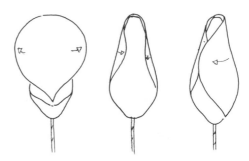

15 Continue to place petals on the rose, not allowing the petals to bend backwards, but allowing them to overlap each other.

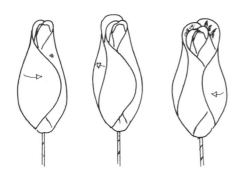

16 Now allow 'air space' to be seen between your petals. As you begin to add the final petals, you will see that they will need to be placed slightly to the side overlapping a previous petal. You may now begin to slightly bend the top of the petals backwards.

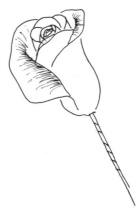

17 Do not be in a hurry to bend petals too far backwards. This is a common fault when making roses, and causes what might have been a good rose to look too artificial. Stop adding petals as soon as the rose looks good. You will find that every rose in the garden is different, and every rose that you make will be different too.

18 Add the calyx whenever you feel the rose looks finished. (See instruction for calyx).

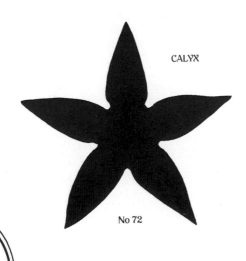

CALYX

No 72

19 Finished rose.

Note: If you wish to continue adding more petals to the rose, remember the size of the cutter will need to be increased, and that the outside petals of the rose become very open and stand away from the centre of the rose. Several petals will be bent backwards.

Full Blown Rose

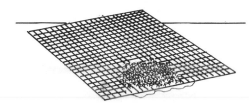

Note: Alternative instructions are given on Page 31 for a cotton centre dipped in yellow vegetable fat. This centre inserted through this cone would be very effective.

1 Tape a firm wire Gauge 22. Bend a hook at the top of the wire. Roll a piece of paste about the size of a marble into a cone shape with a flat top. Place egg white on wire and secure to cone.

2 Now using a piece of fine gauze (available from a hardware shop) press moulding paste through the gauze creating a mass of tiny stamens.

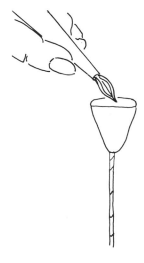

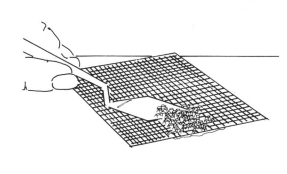

3 Using a paint brush, tip the flat top of the cone with egg white.

4 Lift up all the pieces of tiny stamens with a palette knife.

5 Place carefully in the centre of the cone.

6 Now dip the top of the cone into non-toxic coloured chalk which has been mixed with maize meal to look like pollen.

Full Blown Rose

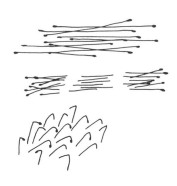

7 Cut many stamens into three, and bend over the heads as illustrated. Use a closed pair of scissors or other tool to help form a crease in the stamen.

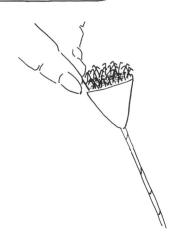

8 Now carefully place numerous stamens around the centre of the cone.

9

Note: An alternative centre for the full brown rose is to make a cotton centre, following the instructions for the Briar Rose, see page 31. Add an additional cotton centre to this with shorter cotton for the middle stamens. Tape together. Pull this cotton centre through the paste cone base. Now colour white vegetable fat yellow. Melt the fat over hot water. Dip the cotton stamens into the yellow fat. Separate with a pin, and then dip the stamens into 'pollen'. This will give you a very attractive effect.

10 Cut out five or six petals using Cutter No. 29. Use Tool No. 3A to soften the edges.

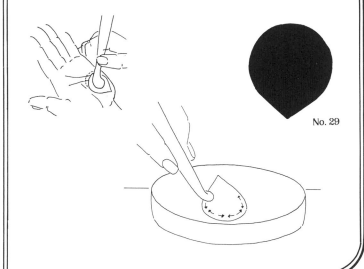

No. 29

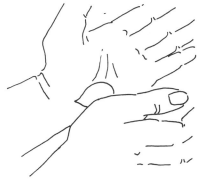

11 Vein petals by pressing palms together.

12 Allow petals to partially dry over artist's plastic palette before attaching to centre cone.

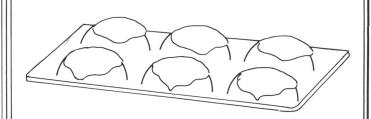

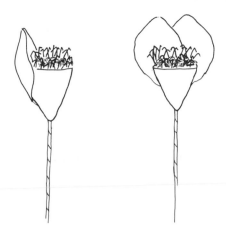

13 When adding each new petal, place it behind the one you have just added. Allow the inside petals to bend slightly inwards.

14 Continue to build up rose, encouraging petals to curl inwards.

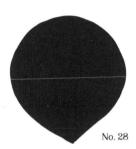

No. 28

16 Cut out more petals using Cutter No. 27. Use Tool 6A to soften the edges. Allow to dry partially. Place in position on flower giving flower an open appearance. Use extra large cutter B23 for final row of petals. Use cocktail stick to curl petals backwards. Petals should be partially dried over convex shape before attaching to flower

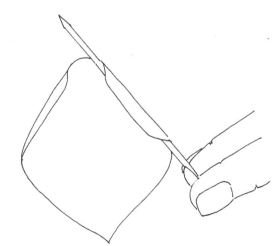

15 Now using Cutter No 28, roll out and cut more petals. Work them very well, remembering to vein them with crêpe paper, or between your palms. Place petals on rose carefully, allowing the rose to fall into place as naturally as possible. Remember to allow 'air' space between petals. Encourage petals to curl away from the centre cone.

B23

B27

Note: When completely dry, add a calyx, using Cutter No 72.

Tiger Lily

Note: The colouring of the stamens will depend on the colour of the tiger lily you are making. A simple guide would be:

Pink – white stamens – brown tips
Yellow – green stamens – brown tips
Orange – pale orange stamens – brown tips

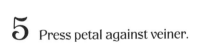

1 Use No. 26 gauge wire, 10cm long, taped in white tape to form the pistil, which should be about 45mm long. Make a small three sided head slightly larger than the stem for the head of the pistil. Shade wire to desired colour of pistil.

2 Make six wire stamens using 30 gauge covered white wire, shade to desired colour with petal dust. Make the anthers, by rolling tiny pieces of light brown paste into thin sausages and attach them to the end of the stamens using gum glue.

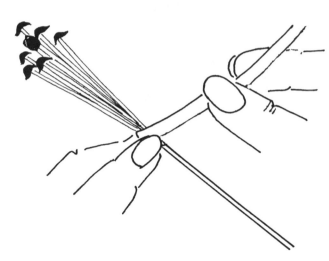

3 Place pistil in centre of stamens and tape together using quarter width florist tape.

4 Using Cutter B24, roll out paste thinly for top of petal but allow paste at base to remain fairly thick for the insertion of very fine, taped, hooked, fuse wire into the petals.

5 Press petal against veiner.

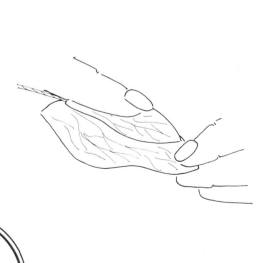

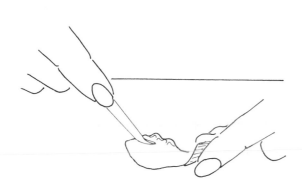

6 Lightly flute edges with tool 2B or 4A.

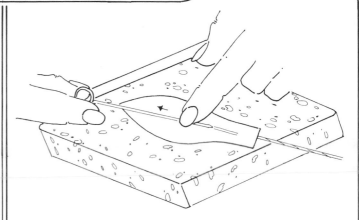

7 Place the petals on a piece of foam. Using a tiny skewer, or a darning needle, pull the skewer over the middle of the petal, beginning at the base and working to the top.

8 Paint in dots using a cocktail stick and a little petal dust mixed with a drop of alcohol.

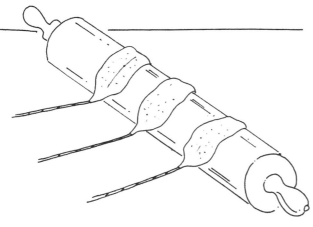

If you wish the petals to curl backwards, dry all six petals over a roller.

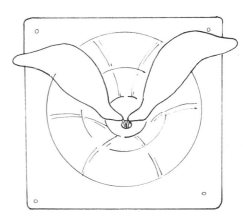

9 If you require a lily with more upright petals, place three petals in flower former No. 4B at equal distances apart. Please note the petals must not be joined together or touch each other at this stage. The petals must be dry before assembling the flower.

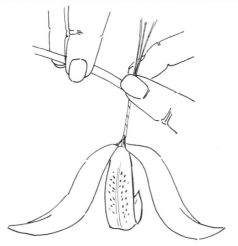

10 Now using half width florist tape, join the three dry petals together, making sure they are evenly spaced and secure. If you are making the very open tiger lily, tape the final row of curled back petals between the first row.

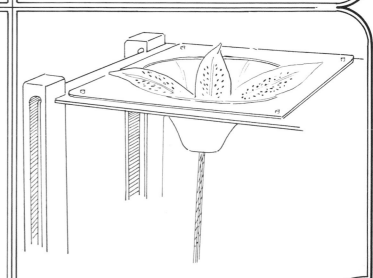

11 Return the flower to flower support 4B.

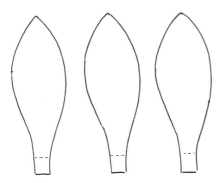

12 Now cut out three more petals using the same cutter as before. You may find it necessary to slightly trim the length of these petals by removing ± 2 mm from the base of the petals. Petals should be thin. Vein and frill petals as before, and colour appropriately.

Note: The use of wire in these three petals is optional. Wiring the petals will mean they have to be dry before assembling. (See Step 9). Finally, the pistil should be added to the petals.

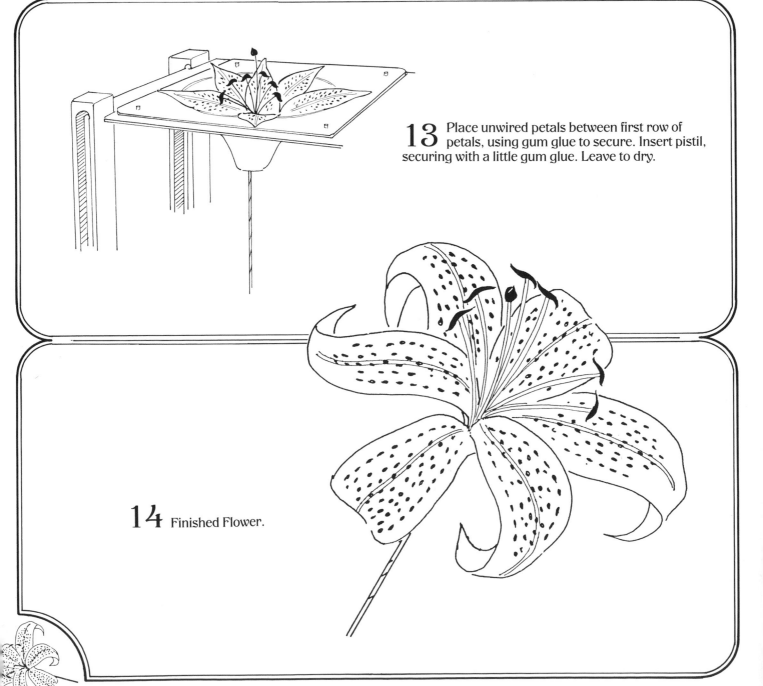

13 Place unwired petals between first row of petals, using gum glue to secure. Insert pistil, securing with a little gum glue. Leave to dry.

14 Finished Flower.

Baby Booties

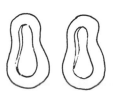 

No 60

No 59

1 Using Cutter No. 60, cut out sole as thickly as possible. Cut a left and a right sole, by simply turning over the paste for one shoe.
Using Tool No. 3B, slightly hollow out centre of sole.

2 Using Cutter 59, cut out tops of bootie.

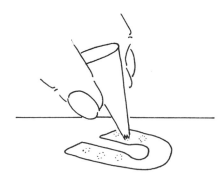

3 Take a small star tube and press in impression on paste to give pattern effect.

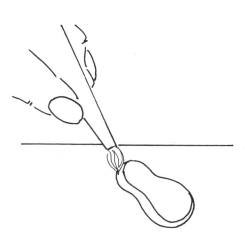

4 Lightly paint egg white around sole of shoe.

5 Top of shoe will fit neatly over sole, slightly overlapping at back of bootie.

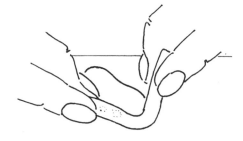

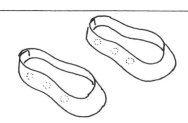

6 Complete both booties to this stage.

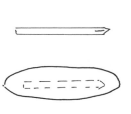

7 Roll out and cut a thin strip for strap. Make a minute incision to form button hole.

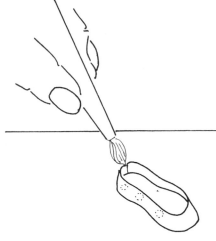

8 Place a little egg white at back of bootie.

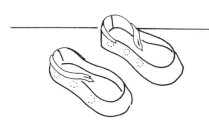

9 Place straps in position. Remember to make a left and a right foot by placing straps opposite each other.

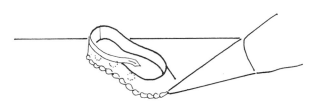

10 Using a No. 0 tube, pipe a fine 'snails trail' around the base of bootie.

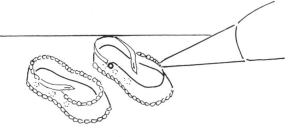

11 Now repeat 'snails trail' around the top of bootie. Remember the button for each bootie.

12 Using Cutter No. 67, cut out baby daisies. Press tool 2A into each petal.

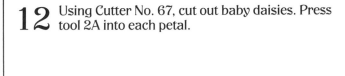

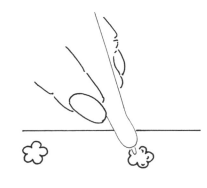

No. 67

13 Place flower on foam and using Tool No. 2A, press in the centre, causing flower to 'cup'.

14 Put a little egg white in the centre of the bootie.

15 Place a flower in the centre of each bootie.

Garrett Frill

Note: Use plastic icing/fondant for this frill. Your cake would probably have been covered with the same plastic icing/fondant.

1 Sieve a little cornflour on a board.

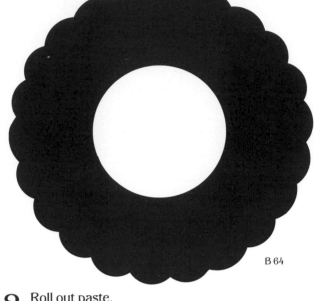

B 64

2 Roll out paste.
Using cutter No. B64, cut out frill.

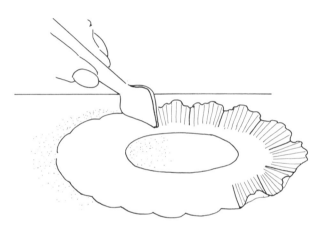

3 Using Tool 5B or a toothpick, carefully press the same number of strokes into each scallop. All the strokes should be the same length. Seven is usually the number of strokes used in each scallop.

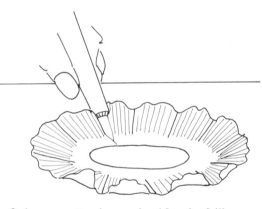

4 Only one cutter is required for the frill. You will use all the scallops for a big frill and simply cut out some of the scallops to reduce the frill to the size you need.

5 Only when you have finished working the whole frill should you cut open the circle. This will enable you to make the incision at a weak spot should one occur, or to cut the frill to the required size.

6 Prepare a pattern to fit the cake and using a pin, carefully mark cake to receive frill. Use egg white on the back of frill and attach to cake. A toothpick will help you to neaten attachment.

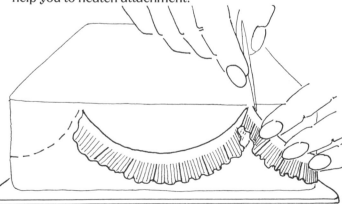

Note: To neaten join, pipe a fine 'snails trail' with either a No 1 or No 0 tube on the inside edge of the frill, making the tube work look like stitches.

Single Bow

1 Begin with a straight piece of ribbon

2 Make a loop in the ribbon.

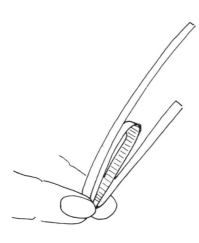

3 Now bring both ends up together on the same side.

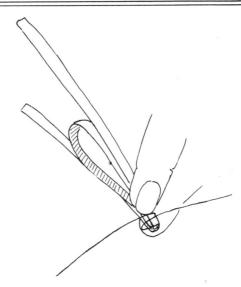

4 Firmly grip ribbon and secure with fine fuse wire.

5 Ribbon secured with fine wire.

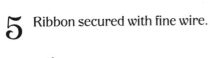

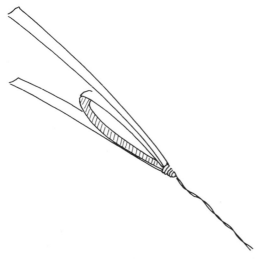

6 Cover the wire with half width florist tape.

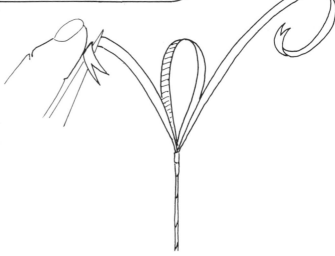

7 Cut out centre of ribbon ends, using small sharp scissors.

8 Holding the blade of scissors against ribbon, pull ribbon against blade of scissors. Ribbon will curl.

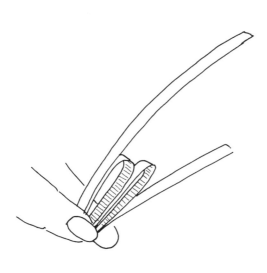

9 To make a double loop, lift up both ends. Secure base with fine fuse wire.

10 Tape securely. Use scissors to trim and curl as above.

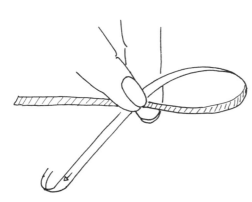

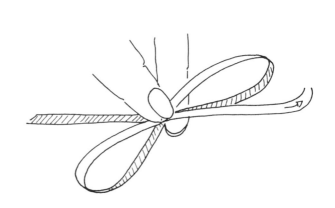

11 Follow diagrams to illustrate the step-by-step build up of a multi-loop bow.

12

Tulle

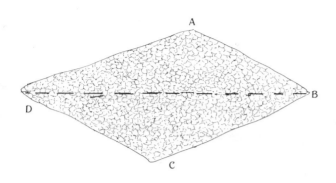

1 Cut small squares of tulle about 6 cm × 6 cm.

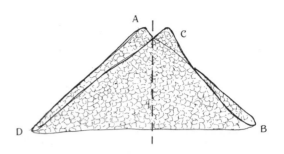

2 Bring corner C up to slightly right of corner A.

3 Now fold corners B and D up towards A and C.

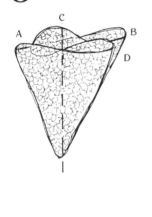

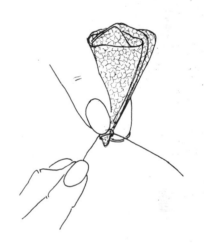

4 Thread fine wire through the base of the tulle.

5 Hook wire securely.

6 Twist wire to ensure tulle is firmly gripped.

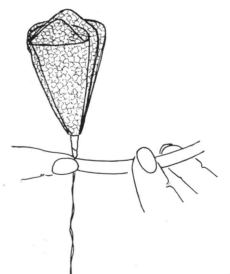

7 Tape to secure and to hide wire.

$\mathcal{C}$orsage

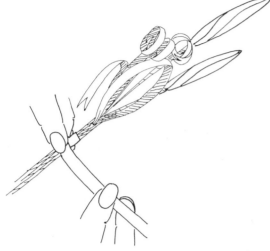

1 Begin with two pointed buds, eg. frangipani, and a single bow ribbon. Tape to secure.

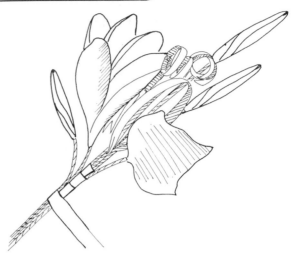

2 Add a flower, eg. frangipani, a leaf and another bud. Tape.

3 Now add flower to opposite sides of stem and another ribbon. Tape.

4 Finally add 2 more leaves, another bud and a final flower. Tape.

Victorian Posy

Note: You will need:
20 single bow ribbons
8 tulle squares
16 leaves
8 small sprays
14 small flowers
16 rose buds
1 centre rose

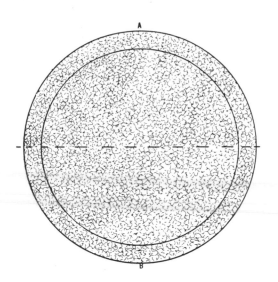

1 Cut two small circles out of tulle in the colour of your choice ± 12 cm in diameter.
The inside circle should be 1 cm smaller than the other.

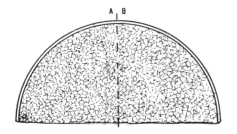

2 Fold tulle in half.

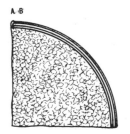

3 Fold tulle in half again.

4 Using small sharp scissors, cut out scallops in tulle.

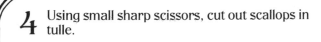

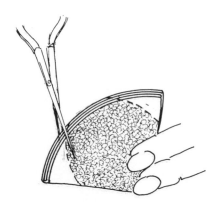

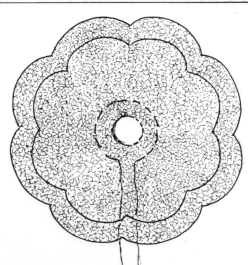

5 With a needle and cotton, stitch around centre circle, leaving two threads of cotton to pull.
Cut out tiny centre of tulle.

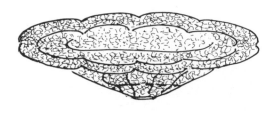

6 Gently pull cotton threads together and tie securely. Place a little plastic icing/fondant in the base of the tulle posy holder to give ballast.

7 Place taped single bow ribbons evenly around the posy. Ease wire into fondant. Add a rose bud and a leaf between each ribbon.

8 Now add tulle between the bud and the leaf. Add a row of small single flowers and sprays next to the tulle.

9 Add more ribbons, rose buds and leaves. Add a row of single flowers around the middle of the posy.

10 Finally add centre rose.

CRESCENT BOUQUET

Note: Repeat the following instructions simultaneously – forming a right and a left side to the crescent. All flowers and leaves should be finely wired and taped.

1 Prepare a ribbon. Attach to a fine, taped wire.

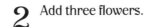

2 Add three flowers.

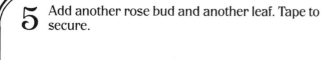

3 Tape to secure.

4 Now add another flower, eg. rose bud. Tape to secure.

5 Add another rose bud and another leaf. Tape to secure.

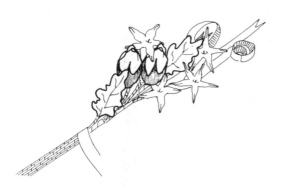

6 Add a small piece of wired tulle and another single ribbon.

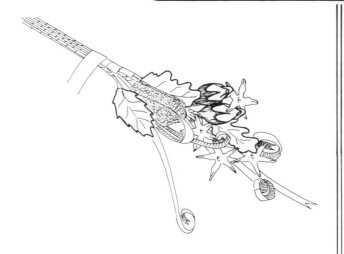

7 Add another leaf and tape to secure.

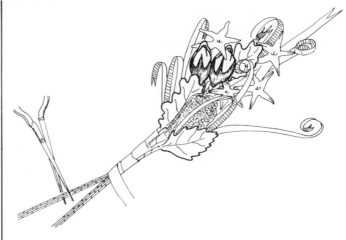

8 Cut out surplus stem wire using wire cutters.

9 Add additional flower, eg. daisy.

10 To make the centre of the crescent, use a full bow to begin with.

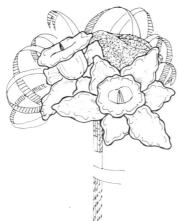

11 Place focal point in position, e.g. daffodils. Add tulle. Tape.

12 Now add three small flowers. Tape to secure.

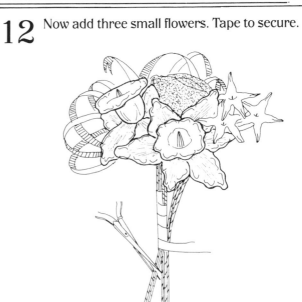

13 Add three rose buds or other flowers. Tape.

14 Add more flowers and leaves to centre. Add more tulle. Tape.

15 Add three daisies, or other flowers. Add more tulle and leaves if necessary. Try to balance the arrangement.

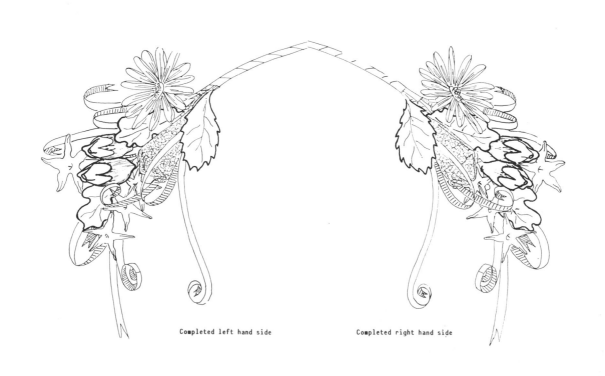

Completed left hand side

Completed right hand side

16

17 Tape centre to sides securely.
Finished crescent.

Note: The use of tulle is optional.

Bridal Bouquet

Note: To make this bouquet you will need at least:-

25-30 – single flowers
15-20 – other single flowers, or feathered carnations.
 7-10 – single ribbons
 7-10 – wired pieces of tulle
 1   – full bow
 1-3 – orchid, or other flowers to form focal point.

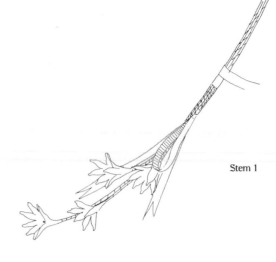

Stem 1

1 Tape together four single flowers and a single ribbon.

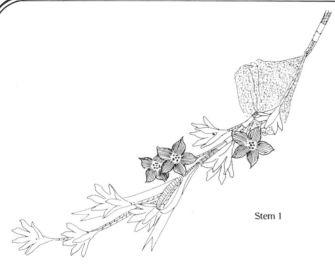

Stem 1

2 Add three different single flowers and three more of the first flower used, together with a piece of tulle. Tape to secure.

Stem 2

3 Tape together two single flowers, then two different flowers, and finally, repeat the first flower used.

4 Add a single ribbon, a piece of tulle and one more of each of the different flowers used.

Stem 2

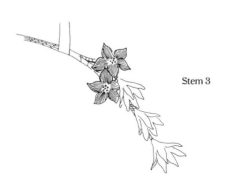

Stem 3

5 Tape three flowers together, then add two of a different type to stem.

Bridal Bouquet

Stem 3

6 Add ribbon, tulle and another flower. Tape securely.

7 Now tape the three stems together, ensuring that they fall in the direction you have planned.

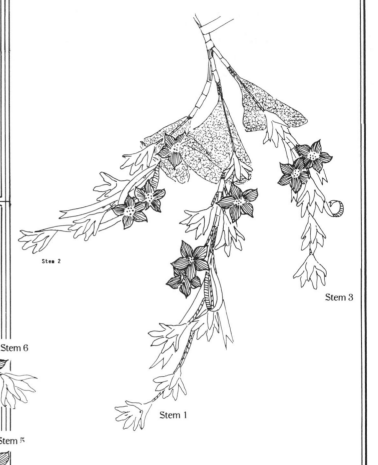

Stem 2

Stem 3

Stem 1

Stem 7

Stem 6

Stem 4

Stem 5

Stem 2

Stem 3

Stem 1

8 Follow illustrations and make Stem 4, Stem 5, Stem 6 and Stem 7 in the same way as the first three stems were made. Tape them together.

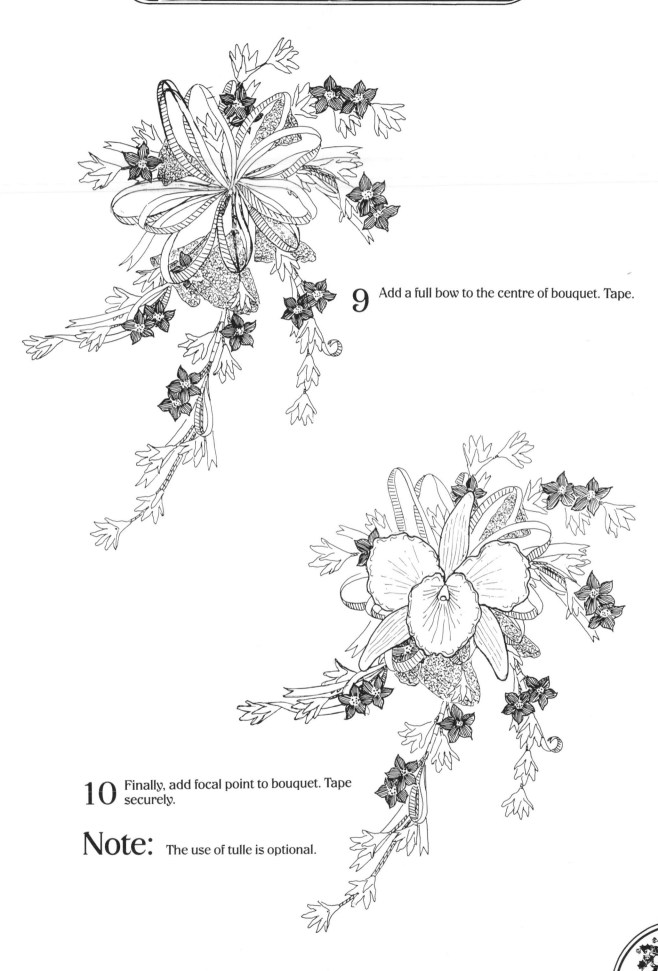

9 Add a full bow to the centre of bouquet. Tape.

10 Finally, add focal point to bouquet. Tape securely.

Note: The use of tulle is optional.

Alternative Methods

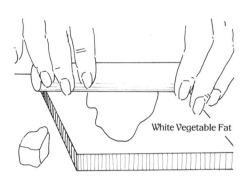

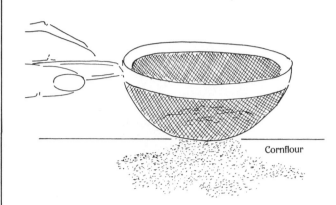

1 Flower paste may be rolled out on a worktop surface lightly spread with white vegetable fat.

2 Flower paste may be rolled out on a worktop surface lightly dusted with cornflour.

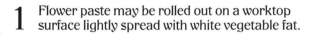

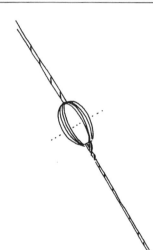

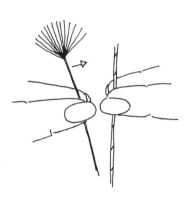

3 Stamens may be made by using sewing cotton rolled into circles over your finger; tightly caught with fine fuse wire; cut appropriately, and joined to stem.

4 Bought stamens may be used and placed into a base of flower paste which has been pressed against some gauze to create a 'stamen' effect.

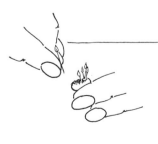

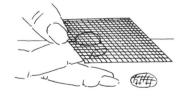

5 A stamen effect may be created by pressing a small ball of paste against a piece of gauze or tulle.

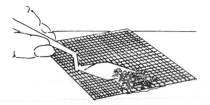

6 Small stamens may be made by forcing paste through gauze.

Petals may be veined by using any of the following methods:

7 crêpe paper

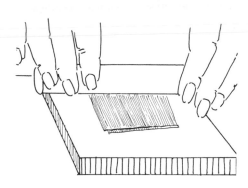

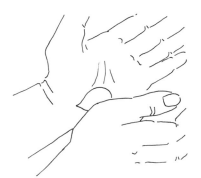

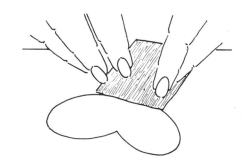

8 pressing your palms together:

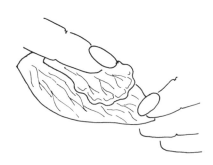

9 plastic tulip petal:

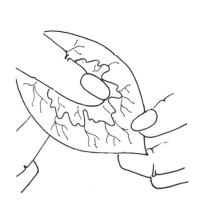

10 rubber leaf veiner:

Alternative Methods

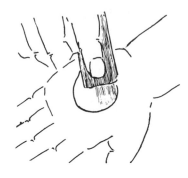

11 dried maize leaf – which has been re-inforced with masking tape to prevent cracking:

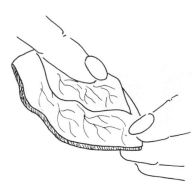

13 moulds made from instant ceramics of flowers and leaves found in the garden – (the hibiscus petal is a very good veiner):

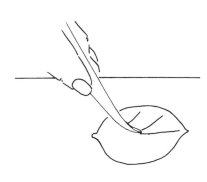

14 Tool No 4B.

15 Leaves may be stemmed by applying gum glue to stem, which is then pressed against the back of the leaf.

16 Roll out leaves, carefully leaving a slight ridge at the centre base of the leaf. A fine, taped, tightly hooked wire is then inserted in the ridge, forming the stem of the leaf.

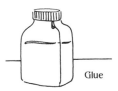
Glue

17 Tylose gum glue is an excellent edible gum glue which should be used in preference to egg white.

18 Egg white may be used to glue petals which are not too large or heavy together, but this method is losing popularity as it goes off too soon.

Egg white

19 Cooking spray gives leaves a realistic sheen.

20 Use a spice bottle and a piece of polystyrene apple box to support flowers. Use 'prestik' to hold in place.

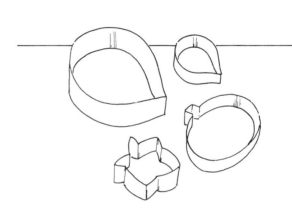

21 Use metal cutters if you have them.

22 The Tilting Turntable Features:
* Packs flat
* Regular turntable
* Stencil features
* Tilting position
* Lazy Susan feature for jars, etc.

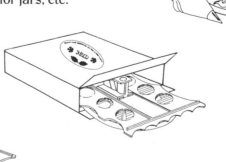

1 Colour a ball of paste to the darkest shade you desire.
Have an equal size ball of paste in white.

2 Cut the coloured ball in half.
Cut the white ball in half.
Reserve half the dark coloured paste and half the white paste.

3 To obtain the medium shade, take half the colour and half the white paste and mix together.

4 Cut the mixed ball of paste in half.

5 To obtain the pale shade, take half the mixed ball and the remaining half of the white paste and mix together.

TYLOSE FLOWER PASTE

Ingredients:
25 ml egg white
250 ml icing sugar
20 ml Tylose C1000P

Method:

Lightly beat egg white. Add sifted icing sugar gradually, mixing all the time, until a soft peak consistency Royal Icing is made. Add the Tylose. The mixture will immediately thicken. Rub white vegetable fat on your hands and work paste thoroughly before working or storing. Place in a plastic bag.

If paste is too firm, work a little extra egg white into it. If paste is too soft, add a little icing sugar. If paste is sticky, rub white vegetable fat on your hands and work paste through very well. It is important to knead paste very well. Seal in a plastic bag in a plastic container.

Paste is ready to use immediately and need not be kept in the fridge. When not in use, may be stored in the fridge.

GUM TRAGACANTH FLOWER PASTE

Ingredients:

2 × 250 ml finely sifted icing sugar
25-30 ml PURE Gum Tragacanth (amount will vary according to climatic conditions).
10 ml gelatin – dissolved in 20 ml cold water (see instructions)
1 egg white beaten with a fork

Method:

1. Pre-heat oven to 100°C and switch off.
2. Using two basins (one oven-proof), rub each very lightly with white vegetable fat. Add 250 ml icing sugar to each basin.
3. In the first basin (oven-proof), add sifted gum tragacanth and mix in well. Place this basin in the oven and allow to warm up.
4. Dissolve gelatin in metal milk warmer, allowing the gelatin to filter through the water. The metal container should be placed in water which has just boiled, but which is not actually boiling.
5. When gelatin is dissolved, add to the heated sugar by making a 'well' in the sugar. Do NOT scrape out surplus gelatin. Stir gently, NOT allowing the 'ball' to break up.
6. Immediately add the lightly beaten egg white, making sure the mixture remains in a single 'ball'.
7. When sugar in the first basin is absorbed, transfer mixture to the second basin.
8. Rub white vegetable fat on your hands. Using your fingers, gently absorb the icing sugar into the wet mixture until you have a pliable mixture which does not stick to your hands.
   * You may not need to use all the sugar in the second basin
   * If paste is too stiff, add a little extra egg white
   * If paste is too soft, add more gum tragacanth
   * Paste should be elastic in texture and should be worked through very well after mixing
   * Store in a plastic bag in a sealed container. Keep in the fridge if not in use.

PLASTIC ICING PASTE

Ingredients:

500 g plastic icing
25 ml gum tragacanth
5 ml egg white

Method:

Add gum tragacanth to plastic icing. Mix in thoroughly.
Add egg white – mix in well.
Rub hands in a little white vegetable fat and continue to work paste until a pliable consistency is achieved.
Store mixture in a plastic bag placed in a sealed plastic container, and keep in the fridge until ready for use.
This paste will improve with age.

(The plastic icing referred to in this recipe is the plastic icing sold to confectioners in South Africa under the Trade name of Pettinice).

TYLOSE GUM GLUE

Use 1 part of Tylose C1000P to 30 parts of water for a substitute for egg white.

If a stronger consistency glue is required, place a little tylose into a container and add a little water to cause the powder to dissolve. Add a little more water gradually until you have the strong consistency you desire.

Kept sealed, this glue lasts for several months.